K-12 Education

Perspectives on the Future

K-12 Education

Perspectives
on the Future

The Van Andel Education Institute
Grand Rapids, Michigan

For all the children

Contents

Foreword   ix

Van Andel Institute   xiii

A Message from the Chairman   xv

Van Andel Educators Institute
An Academic Program

Leaders and Organizations

1 Leadership 1   5
         – Howard E. Gardner

2 What's a Movement?   27
         – Max De Pree

Character and Morals

3 Character Matters I: Contours of Character   35
4 Character Matters II: No Safe Harbor   53
         – Cornelius Plantinga, Jr.

5 Education and the Challenge of Cultural Conflicts
   in a Democratic Society   77
6 Moral Education and American Pluralism   89
         – James Davison Hunter

Motivation for Learning

7 An Engineer's Perspective on K-12 Education   103
8 An Agenda to Engage Research Universities
   in K-12 Education   123
            – Ronald M. Latanision

9 Creating Educational Excellence for Urban Children   139
            – Lisa D. Delpit

Epilogue   159

Suggested Reading   163

1997 Van Andel Educators Institute   164

Foreword

We have attempted the difficult task of transposing thoughtful, stimulating lectures, presented in an environment where there was considerable dialogue and discussion, from the richness of the spoken word to the discipline of the printed page. We believe these lectures are of such quality and significance that these efforts are well warranted. It is our hope that you, the reader, will confirm our judgment and that you will also sense something of the spirit of inquiry and challenge that prevailed.

These lectures were presented at the 1997 Van Andel Educators Institute, held August 4–8, 1997, at Haworth Conference Center on the campus of Hope College in Holland, Michigan. We had the privilege of bringing together seven lecturers from various disciplines and thirty educators who serve as either a superintendent of a school system or a principal of a school. These superintendents and principals came from various parts of the country, from various types of schools—urban, suburban, and rural—and brought with them various personal backgrounds and experiences.

The Educators Institute was the first major undertaking of a newly formed organization, the Van Andel Education Institute. The Education Institute, along with a companion organization, the Van Andel Research Institute, are the operating arms of the Van Andel Institute, founded in 1996 by Jay and Betty Van Andel as the vehicle for accomplishing their major long-term philanthropic goals in education and medical science research.

In 1996, Luis A. Tomatis, a distinguished cardiac surgeon who is president of both the Research and Education Institutes, invited me to play a role in shaping the direction and programs of the Van Andel Education Institute. I had been retired from the presidency of Hope College for nine years, but this was a unique opportunity. I realized that the institute has the potential to play a definitive role in education.

As Dr. Tomatis and I began to chart a course for the activities of the Van Andel Education Institute, we were well aware of the major concerns related to K-12 education and decided that our initial efforts should be focused in this area. We met with a number of national education leaders to seek their counsel on the needs of K-12 education and the role the institute might play.

From these conversations we concluded that the Van Andel Education Institute would focus initially on foundational issues such as the purposes of education, the learning process, moral and ethical issues, leadership, and the scientific and cultural developments in contemporary society that impact K-12 education. It was in this context that the concept for the 1997 Van Andel Educators Institute was developed, which in turn led to the presentation of the lectures recorded here.

The authors of the first two lectures, both gifted in their respective fields, address leadership from quite different perspectives. Howard Gardner, Professor of Education at Harvard University, has written brilliantly on a range of issues and presents a perceptive analysis of various types of leaders. His distinction between direct and indirect leaders provides insights into who is a leader and how leaders function.

Max De Pree writes from a background of forty years in management, including eight as Chairman and CEO of Herman Miller, an office systems manufacturer in Zeeland, Michigan, that is recognized for its excellence in design and is regularly listed as one of the most admired companies in America. He addresses leadership in the context of what marks a successful organization.

Though they express their views of leaders in different terms, both Howard Gardner and Max De Pree emphasize the creativity and competence of strong leaders. They stress the importance of leaders living in accordance with the values they profess.

Various issues involving morals, character, and contemporary culture are addressed in two lectures by Cornelius Plantinga, Dean

of the Chapel at Calvin College in Grand Rapids, and two by James
Hunter, the William R. Kenan Jr. Professor of Sociology and Religious Studies at the University of Virginia. At first glance it may
appear that they have rather sharply conflicting points of view.
Cornelius Plantinga develops the concept of character as a basket-
ful of virtues and goes on to assert that in spite of basic cultural
differences, there is broad basic agreement in our society on the
range of virtues that should be cultivated. James Hunter points
very perceptively to the deep cultural differences that have emerged
in contemporary society that make it difficult, if not impossible, to
achieve a solid basis for unity in our nation.

On reflection, however, these differences do not loom unduly
large, for the agreement on virtues is at an operational level. James
Hunter points out that if we acknowledge the basic differences in
our world views—and do not gloss over them—we are in a much
better position to understand each other and work together for
common goals, even while acknowledging our differences. The issues addressed in these lectures are at the core of many debates in
contemporary society; the insights of these authors are important
contributions to the dialogue.

Ronald Latanision, Professor of Materials Science and Engineering at Massachusetts Institute of Technology, has a keen interest in K-12 education. He looks at K-12 education, applying an
engineering technique for examining any failure—*root cause analysis*. Using this analysis technique on the problems of K-12 education, he concludes that motivation is a key issue that must be addressed. His insights into not only the role of motivation in education but also the importance of educating students so that they
can be effective in their work are important contributions to discussions on the purposes of education.

In the final lecture in this book, Lisa Delpit, the Benjamin E.
Mays Professor of Urban Educational Excellence at Georgia State
University, addresses one of the most important issues we face as a
nation: the education of minority youth, particularly in our large
cities. The insights she presents out of her background of experience

and scholarship are basic and fundamental and, when incorporated into the understanding and practice of teachers, will certainly enhance the learning experiences of all students.

We are deeply grateful to these lecturers for allowing their words to be printed and for their invaluable help in editing them for the printed page. We extend our profound thanks and deep gratitude to them for joining us—a new and unknown organization—in this search for solutions, for their thought-provoking lectures, and for their role in the creative discussions that followed.

It is with genuine appreciation that I express my gratitude to Jane Haradine for her invaluable help in publishing this volume. She provided superb editing and many creative suggestions in bringing this effort to fruition. I also extend thanks to Denise DeJonge for her excellent work in transcribing the lectures. On behalf of all who participated, I extend our thanks to Jay and Betty Van Andel for their vision and generosity, which made this entire project possible.

Gordon J. Van Wylen
Trustee
Van Andel Education Institute

Van Andel Institute

The Van Andel Institute was founded in 1996 by Jay and Betty Van Andel as the vehicle through which they would fulfill their dream of a lasting legacy that will enrich the lives and enhance the health of generations to come. The vision for the institute is rooted in Jay and Betty Van Andel's religious faith and their concern for the well-being of their fellow humans. This is a legacy that their children—Nan, Steven, David, and Barbara—are committed to perpetuating.

As a cofounder of Amway, Jay Van Andel brought clarity of vision and great personal energy to this very successful endeavor. He served as chairman of the U.S. Chamber of Commerce and as North American chairman of the Netherlands American Bicentennial Commission.

Betty Van Andel played a major role in advancing the arts in West Michigan and in bringing Opera Grand Rapids into the limelight. She served on the board of Pine Rest Christian Hospital, one of the largest mental health centers in West Michigan.

The generosity of Jay and Betty Van Andel to a wide range of institutions and cultural endeavors in the Grand Rapids area has greatly enriched the quality of life for residents. Through the Van Andel Institute, their compassion and concern for others will have new dimensions and embrace both national and international perspectives.

The Van Andel Institute is dedicated to two major fields: medical science research and education. The medical science research will be conducted through the Van Andel Research Institute (VARI). A five-member Board of Scientific Advisors, four of whom are Nobel Laureates, has been appointed to guide the activities of VARI. A major research facility, designed by the distinguished architect Raphael Vinoly, is under construction in Grand Rapids on the

campus of Butterworth Hospital. This facility will house the initial research activities, which will focus on molecular biology and
genetics, and include clinical research.

The Van Andel Education Institute is dedicated to making
definitive contributions to achieving excellence in education. Its
initial emphasis is on foundational issues of education, such as the
learning process, the purposes of education, the impact of technology and cultural developments on education leadership, and the
moral, ethical, and character issues that bear on education. The
institute's initial activity was the 1997 Van Andel Educators Institute, at which the lectures published in this book were presented.

Each of the three institutes—Van Andel Institute, Van Andel
Research Institute, and Van Andel Education Institute—is gov-
erned by a board of directors. David Van Andel, a senior vice president at Amway, serves as Chairman of the Board and CEO of each
of the institutes. Luis A. Tomatis, recently retired after a distinguished career as a cardiac surgeon, serves as President and COO
of the Research and Education Institutes. David Van Andel and
Luis Tomatis are both deeply committed to the vision of Jay and
Betty Van Andel and to ensuring that their dream of enriching the
lives of future generations is fulfilled with distinction and honor.

A Message from the Chairman

As my parents have moved along in years, they have searched for ways to give something positive and meaningful back to the community and to society at large. The Van Andel Institute was created to enable them to do just that.

Our family has long been aware of the importance of good education, not only for personal fulfillment but also for the key role that education plays in helping us all become responsible citizens in the communities where we live and work. Over the years we have provided financial support for Christian education and for higher education at several institutions. Our present focus is on basic education—K-12 education.

We are very grateful to the 1997 Van Andel Educators Institute lecturers and participants for the way, in one short week, they brought focus and perceptive insights into a range of issues of vital importance to education. The lectures presented were outstanding and it is a privilege to be able to publish them.

We offer this book to you, hoping that by making this information available to a wider audience, the insights presented under the institute's banner at that first gathering of educators will become a positive factor in efforts to enhance and strengthen K-12 education. Improving education for all children is one of the most significant endeavors that we as a nation can undertake and in which we as individuals can be involved.

David Van Andel
Chairman
Van Andel Institute

Van Andel Educators Institute

An Academic Program

Leaders
and Organizations

Photo © Jerry Bauer, 1994

Dr. Howard E. Gardner
Professor of Education
Graduate School of Education
Harvard University
Cambridge, Massachusetts

Dr. Howard E. Gardner is Professor of Education, Adjunct Professor of Psychology, and Co-Director of Project Zero at Harvard University.

He is the author of numerous books and monographs, many of which have been translated into other languages. His work on multiple intelligences is particularly well known.

Dr. Gardner has received many awards and often is called to serve on national boards and committees.

He received both his A.B. and Ph.D. degrees from Harvard University.

Howard E. Gardner

Chapter 1

Leadership 1

Let me begin with the famous Teheran Conference of November 1943. Josef Stalin, Franklin Roosevelt, and Winston Churchill met for the first time and planned the fates of millions of people during the concluding phase of World War II. When most individuals think about leaders, they have in mind prototypical individuals like them.

We do not usually think of Einstein as a leader. But I want to argue that, in interesting ways, men like Einstein are leaders. What Einstein has in common with the Teheran crowd is having enormous influence on people and events. Indeed, if you think about the denouement of the Second World War and the fifty years afterwards, it's arguable that Einstein had as much influence as did the trio of leaders at Teheran. Not only did Einstein have the idea that led to the atomic weapons which ended the Second World War, but the postwar period was dominated by the nuclear threat.

It may seem even a further stretch to think of a Chinese drawing teacher in the city of Chengdu as a leader. But I am going to ask you to think about the political leaders of the world, the intellectual leaders of the world, the educational leaders of the world, and the foot soldiers of the world as all being leaders in a certain sense. They are all engaged in the project of changing mental representations and transforming the way the individuals with whom they come in contact think about things and go about doing things.

⁕

This paper and the others printed in this book were delivered orally at the Van Andel Educators Institute at Hope College in August 1997. They have been edited only in the interest of clarity.

What is a leader?

A leader is an individual who significantly affects others—
their thoughts, feelings, and behaviors. Leaders accomplish their
mission in two primary ways. They tell stories and they lead certain kinds of lives. I believe that stories are vitally important for
leaders. Stories have drama. They feature protagonists who are trying to achieve things. There are obstacles, plenty of them.

Leaders tell stories, but it's also important to take note of the
kinds of lives they lead. If leaders tell one story but lead a contradictory life, they're hypocrites. Maybe it's better to be a hypocrite
than to be morally insensate, but ultimately, if you tell one story
but your own life fails to embody it, your leadership is less effective.

Being very fair politically, I will use two quotations from political leaders. One is "I am not a crook." It's hard to say that when
you are, in fact, a crook. Another is "I favor family values." It's hard
to do that if, in fact, you are unfaithful, promiscuous, absent. Stories don't go over in the long run if what people actually do doesn't
live up to their words.

One of the reasons why the story that Churchill told about
England during World War II was so effective was because he seemed
to embody the story in his own courageous, if sometimes outland-
ish, personal stance.

I have a cognitive view of leadership. My distinctive addition
to the literature on leadership is to argue that leadership occurs in
the mind. It occurs in the minds of leaders and followers. The
vehicles of this mental transaction are stories. A leader tells stories;
he hopes that those stories affect what other people do. It would be
easy to be a leader if everybody else's mind were a blank slate—if it
were unpopulated with others' stories. Then you would just tell a
story and it would be accepted or rejected on its merits.

But even by the age of five, everybody has hundreds of stories
in their mind. By the time we're adults, we have thousands of
stories in our mind—some of them we're very conscious of and
some we're not so conscious of. So when a leader tries to tell a story,
he or she must ask: Is anybody going to notice it? Is the story going

to have any impact on anybody? If it's too remote, it's going to be ignored. We all know lecturers who are just too far from where we are, or movies that are too far from where we are, and they have no impact. Most narratives suffer from the opposite problem. They are so familiar (like the average television show) that we have total amnesia the next day; we have heard of thousands of stories like that before.

It's the story that is sufficiently distant—but not so remote that we lose it—that has the potential of actually affecting us.

I see leadership as a Darwinian process where the new stories are competing with the stories already there. Often stories have rivals—what I call counter-stories. For a leader's story to have any effect, it has to slay, to nudge aside, or somehow transform or transmogrify the existing stories. In most situations, identity stories are at a premium. People are very interested in who they are individually and corporately. One of the things that leaders tell us is who we are and what we're aspiring to. We pay particular attention to those identity stories because they convey very important issues to us.

Margaret Thatcher is clearly a leader. She's been one of the most effective leaders of the second half of the twentieth century. But if you're like me, she provokes ambivalent feelings in you. She's a very good example of somebody who's an excellent storyteller and who embodies her story. When she came into power in 1979, her story was this: England had lost its way. Socialism was a bad thing. England was once a great power—a powerful, imperial, fair nation of shopkeepers doing their own stuff, working hard, getting ahead. Instead, the fat Socialists, with the tacit tolerance of the Tories, had formed a post–World War II consensus. England was becoming a minor power, not working very hard; unions were being too powerful and nationalizing all of the industries. Thatcher was going to set England on her right course.

Thatcher not only had a story that England was ready to hear, she also appeared to *embody* that story. She was a self-made person. Her father was not wealthy. She lived above the grocery store which he ran. She went to school and got two advanced degrees on her own. She was the first woman Shadow leader of her party and, of course, the first woman prime minister in British history and, I believe, the longest running prime minister of the century. She was seen as courageous in the Falkland Islands War and after the bombing in Brighton, where she almost lost her life. So, in sum, she looked like the kind of person she was talking about. She wasn't simply a good actor or pretender, she seemed to really walk the talk. I think one of the reasons why Colin Powell appeals to the American people is that he seems to live what he talks about. He's not just somebody who has a good speechwriter or spin controller.

That's what's distinctive about a cognitive view of leadership. You really have to engage the counter-stories, show where they are inadequate, what's wrong, say, with the Labor position in postwar England. You have to make people feel that the position you are taking in your story and in the life you are holding as a model is really a much more effective way of going about the thing. The leaders whom we admire, whether it's Martin Luther King, Jr., or Nelson Mandela, are people who really showed us how our versions had inadequacies. They show us not just by being persuasive but by living a certain kind of life. Gandhi led a life which made it very clear to his followers what kind of human beings they ought to be.

A study of leaders

I did a study with Emma Laskin that was reported in my book *Leading Minds*. I carried out biographical studies of twenty-one leaders, including ten who were leaders during the Second World War. They all came from this century. They didn't just tell familiar stories (I would call such a person a manager of an organization). I'm interested in people who changed the way other people are, not people who simply reinforced current habits or ideas. The people in the study were *voluntary* in the sense that they were persuasive; they did not compel agreement through force. My sample was also skewed toward individuals who tell inclusionary stories— stories that involve many people in their "we." Actually, it turns out that being inclusionary is not necessarily advantageous for a leader; sometimes it is more effective to be exclusionary, to characterize individuals as being outside of your chosen circle.

Let me mention whom I studied. Two people led scholarly domains: Margaret Mead, the anthropologist, and Robert Oppenheimer, the physicist who actually put Einstein's ideas into practice by leading the Manhattan Project. I will later call these people *indirect* leaders who tried to become *direct* leaders. These people led by the force of their ideas.

Then I studied people who led circumscribed institutions, among them Robert Maynard Hutchins, a very effective leader of the University of Chicago in the 1930s and 1940s. One of the ways that we know that he was effective is that fifty years after Hutchins stopped being president, the University of Chicago still bears the shadow of his contributions.

I studied people who led what I call the classical estates. Alfred Sloan was the extremely successful head of General Motors. When he had an organization, he went around the country and talked with the people who ran the different franchises. George Marshall led an even bigger estate called the U.S. Army. There were 8.5 million soldiers under Marshall in the Second World War. Pope John XXIII led a group of about one billion people called the Catholic Church.

Note that these people inherited organizations or institutions. This is extremely important for the area of schools. One reason why it is much easier to form a new school is because you are creating a new organization. You're not trying to change an organization that already exists. In a sense, a new school has a much easier time becoming a movement. Sloan, Marshall, and Pope John XXIII led classical estates, and so they're very different from Eleanor Roosevelt and Martin Luther King, Jr., two leaders—of women and African Americans, respectively—who didn't have any organizations. They had to create organizations.

Leadership is entirely different when you don't have a group and you have to create one. The dynamics between people who already have expectations, who already know a certain story, differ from the dynamics which govern people who need to create new

stories. Creating a new story is a much, much more difficult problem, and it's much harder to sustain your efforts once you've passed
from the scene.

I studied one leader of a nation—Margaret Thatcher—and I
examined two people who sought to lead beyond national boundaries. Mahatma Gandhi, of course, the leader of Indian independence, had enormous impact in the United States, South Africa,
China, Russia, and so on. And I studied a person who has had
enormous influence on this century and whose influence actually
grows every day, Jean Monnet. Monnet was the French economist
who had the idea of the European Union, the Common Market,
and who worked for sixty years to try to get it started, and at last he
appears to be crowned with success.

As sort of a control group for my more intensive studies, I also
examined ten leaders from World War II, including Hitler,
Mussolini, Roosevelt, Stalin, and Chiang Kai-Shek.

The intelligences of a leader

I want to relay just a few findings from this large study. A first
finding concerns the intelligences of the leader. Given what I've
said, there are three intelligences which are important for a leader.
One is linguistic because leaders have to tell stories. Occasionally
they can do it in another symbol system, but by and large they do
it in words, orally, although sometimes in writing. They need interpersonal intelligence—an understanding of other people—because leaders try to get people to change the way they are. You
can't do that if you don't understand other people. I think leaders
also traffic in existential intelligence because they help us understand who we are. They answer these existential questions of what
are our goals, what are the obstacles, why are we here, why do we
live, why do we die?

One interesting thing is that leaders don't particularly have
logical mathematical intelligence. In fact, there's a study that shows
a negative correlation between understanding of economics and
being a good leader. Interestingly, Ronald Reagan was consistently

underestimated throughout his life because he wasn't a particularly logical character. He was, in fact, a brilliant storyteller. In Washington most people are lawyers and they are logical; many of them thought that Reagan was a fool. But Reagan wasn't trafficking in that particular commodity. It wasn't important for his being a leader.

Leaders take risks, defy authority

An early marker of leadership is that, when they're young, leaders take risks and defy authority. They are willing to confront people in authority, not necessarily in an in-your-face way, but more to say, "I've analyzed the situation and I see it somewhat differently, and this is how I see it." If they're too in-your-face, they would get killed or marginalized. The trick is to do it in a way where you're taken seriously.

The best example of that is George Marshall, who was not a particularly aggressive character. In fact, he was rather taciturn as military people go. The first time he met General [John] Pershing during the First World War and the first time he met Franklin Roosevelt before the Second World War, he told them off in public—an incredible thing to do. In fact, Secretary of the Treasury Henry Morgenthau said to Marshall, "Nice knowing you, George," because you didn't tell Roosevelt off in public the first time you met him and survive. But, in fact, in both cases Marshall was hired immediately afterward to be chief of staff. So there is something about the way that these people can take risks and confront authority which is a marker of a future leader.

Now, to anticipate my story a bit, I said to myself, *"Well, people like Einstein or Oppenheimer or Margaret Mead didn't confront authority, and so maybe they're not leaders."* But, in fact, I didn't take my own analysis seriously enough. Indirect leaders tell their stories through the work they do. What you'll find with creative people who are indirect leaders is that they are telling off the people in authority, but they do it *through their work.* Einstein didn't have to tell his professor off. He simply rendered his professor irrelevant by his own analysis of time and space. As did Picasso with his paintings, and Schönberg and Stravinsky and the Beatles with their music. So there is a defying of authority and risk-taking among indirect leaders, but it doesn't occur face-to-face; it occurs through the actual iconoclastic work that they do.

Leadership is very different if you inherit an organization with stories and norms than if you're creating a movement. If you don't have an organization, a lot of your energy has to be devoted toward creating one with some stability. Many people think that the Internet will be the locus of new power in organizations. I'm actually very skeptical because, to put it bluntly, it's too easy to drop out of the Internet. People would have to establish norms where you couldn't do that and, of course, that goes against the spirit of the Internet.

Leaders need opportunities for reflection. The interesting thing is that indirect leaders or creators—the Einstein types—really spend about 90 percent of their time reflecting and about 10 percent of their time meeting the rest of the world and making sure that what they're thinking isn't crazy. With people who are more direct leaders—like superintendents or principals—90 percent of your time is spent with other people, and that's probably necessary, but that last 10 percent of your time is really crucial. If you don't have time to reflect and see the big picture, you are very vulnerable to costly mistakes. I worry about people who spend all their nights going out, who don't have vacations, including vacations for thinking.

Leaders try and fail

Finally, leaders are not people who succeed all the time. In fact, most leaders fail more than the rest of us because they are very ambitious and far-reaching and because they're trying to change things. Their lives are dotted with failures. Where they differ, at least from me if not from you, is in the way they frame the things that don't go well.

If you're dealing with a group of experts, a homogeneous group that knows a lot about your topic, then you can talk with a fairly sophisticated story. When economists meet or when the Bar

Association meets, the stories that are conveyed are pretty complicated. However, most leaders are facing heterogeneous groups, groups which, even though they may have experts, feature individuals who aren't experts in the same thing. With heterogeneous groups, stories need to be very simple because they are basically addressed to the unschooled mind. I got interested in leadership because Gandhi was so different from the other creative people whom I'd studied; he was dealing with an unschooled mind and a heterogeneous group.

I had thought that it was always good to have the big "we" and to have a very inclusionary story. But there's a risk, in fact. The broader the "we," the more that people who are your core constituents don't feel special anymore. They feel alienated. They feel they've been neglected. Margaret Thatcher, in fact, got very far by being exclusionary. Her favorite question was "Is he or she one of us?" with the obvious implication: if not, "off with his or her head." She was very oppositional and found that to be a very productive stance. It's no accident that leaders like Gandhi and Yitzhak Rabin were assassinated not by people from outside their circle but by people from inside their core groups who felt that they were not being a good enough Hindu or a good enough Jew. Similarly, Martin Luther King's loss of influence occurred when he stopped having African Americans from the South as his core constituency, moved toward poor people in general, moved his operations to the North, and shifted to political issues like the Vietnam War. Then people who could speak more directly to his earlier constituencies—Stokely Carmichael, Rap Brown, and Malcolm X—became the more effective exclusionary kinds of leaders.

A leader and authenticity

Finally, the most effective stories grow out of the life of the leader. They have an authenticity because the narrative represents experiences he or she has gone through and has grappled with. The opposite side of the coin occurs when you try to tell a story that somebody else has written for you. In the long run, it won't be convincing because your own life won't embody that story. In fact,

I think the best stories grow out of lifelong embodiments. This doesn't mean that you have to be like everybody else. But it does mean that not only does your story have to be authentic, it has to touch on certain aspects of your constituency even if, in superficial aspects, they are very different from you and from one another.

I was in a meeting where many of the leaders of the world were in attendance, many influential people like Bill Gates [co-founder and CEO of Microsoft]. Everybody wanted to see Bill Gates because he's admired so widely nowadays. But there was one leader who, when he walked into the meeting, everybody stood up for automatically. This was Nelson Mandela. Most people in that room had little in common with Nelson Mandela except that he's a human being, and they knew they could connect to him on the human level. When Nelson Mandela got sworn in as president of South Africa, he had his jailer sitting in the first row. That's such a Gandhian touch.

If you're a leader and you want to have a formidable challenge, try to tell a story about downsizing. When I meet with business leaders, I actually give them that assignment because it concentrates the mind very well. Somebody raised that same question yesterday. They said, "What do we tell our constituents when we have a budget that's cut by 20 percent? What do we tell our teachers? What do we tell our parents? What do we tell our kids?" Those are the times that try leaders' souls.

Going back to the Bible and probably to prehistory, the leaders conveyed stories. Incidentally, because Moses wasn't able to talk very well, he had to hire a storyteller, his brother Aaron, but most of us don't have that luxury. Charles Darwin did. Darwin had a colleague named Huxley who could go on the hustings, and that turned out to be very important. Do leaders embody their story? Christ is one seamless embodiment. Do they have an audience? And how do they create and maintain one, particularly if their story is jarring? What is their organizational and institutional base? How do they maintain it and keep it from regressing into being a mere organization rather than a place with productive tension that is at least in part a movement?

I'm going to make a provocative statement here. Whether you're a third-grade teacher or a high school principal or the superintendent of a small or large district, there are several trends in the world that are going to affect what you do. One is the knowledge we all have that the world could be destroyed by a bomb or an asteroid or some combination thereof. This used to be true religiously; now we know it's true scientifically as well. Another is the fact of instant communication, often simplistic. With the Internet, everybody in the world knows it if it's of interest. There is a lack of privacy. There is a rise of global, transnational entities which have more and more control over lives. When Gates and [House Speaker Newt] Gingrich get together, Gates is seen as having the power. International organizations are really where it's at, whether they're business or governmental or non-governmental. This gives rise in our country and in other ones as well to new fundamentalisms, to tribalisms, as people can't deal with these large entities and these very large trends. According to one study, the only group of Americans that is optimistic about the future is the two million readers of *Wired* magazine, which deals with the Internet. One might want to ponder that. They're not threatened by the future because they represent the future. But for those of us who don't read or understand *Wired,* the future is threatening, and one way to deal with threat is to stand very firm on your own tribal foundation.

Every area is becoming more technical. To get ahead, you have to be an expert. I always say if you survive to sixty, then you can be a generalist. But earlier, all the rewards come from becoming more and more of an expert in a narrow enterprise. Everything is technical nowadays. But at the same time, leaders have to tell stories that are simple because the groups are heterogeneous. Members won't understand a complicated story. [President Bill] Clinton and Thatcher are both fantastic storytellers. I always say that the problem with Clinton is that he tells too many stories and it's not clear which ones he believes. But Clinton and Thatcher are both sophisticated enough to understand the technical aspects, so they can do some translation. Most of us don't understand the technical aspects, so we repeat somebody else's version, which is dangerous.

Or we understand the technical aspects very well and, like most academics, we tell stories that are too complicated. All leaders need to wrestle with these forces, which I think are more pressing now than they would have been even thirty years ago.

Indirect leaders

I want now to return to Einstein, Mead, Stravinsky, Freud, and other people whom we would call creators. I call them *indirect* leaders. Both indirect leaders and direct leaders are trying to influence people. But indirect leaders do it through works that they create, what I would call symbolic products: pieces of paper with squiggles on them, whether they're drawings or scores of music or poetry or scientific theories or big fat books about intelligence. That's the means whereby the influence is wrought or not wrought. Don't think that indirect leaders are less powerful than direct leaders.

One could argue the reverse. The economist John Maynard Keynes said something very profound. He said, in effect, "Don't make fun of dead economists. The world is ruled by the ideas of dead economists which are put into practice by people who had never heard of the economists."

Indirect leaders are very powerful, but you may not know them. It doesn't matter to science what Einstein looked like, what he talked about to his friends, or even, to be frank, whether he loved his wife. What matters is the quality of the symbols that he created and whether they influenced other physicists. Indirect leaders deal with other experts in their domain, other physicists, other composers. They lead by creating products which affect the work of other people in their domains, which in turn change the domains: their embodiment is how they go about doing their work. People learn about how Einstein thinks, and that's very important for people who want to continue to be physicists.

And the same thing happens to anybody who is an indirect kind of leader. Because you're dealing with experts, the stories or the products that they deal with can be quite sophisticated. Therefore, creators contrast with *direct* leaders, those who work with groups that are heterogeneous, that are spoken to directly. Because direct leaders are dealing with unschooled minds, their stories have to be simple. The simple stories drive out the complex stories. In a struggle, the simple stories always win initially.

What is creativity?

My definition of creativity parallels my definitions of intelligence. Intelligence entails having "computers" that work very well with one or more kind of contact. If you're linguistically intelligent, you've got a good language computer which processes language easily and you can learn language quickly. If you have a good musical computer, you can process musical stuff efficiently and learn music easily. Prodigies are people who just have computers that are better than the rest of us. Experts are people whose computers operate well, either because God blessed them, their genes blessed them, or because they had very good teaching. It doesn't matter. But experts are people with high intelligence or intelligences. They are different from creators.

Creators are people who regularly solve problems. People are not creative only once in their life. It's a regular mode of being, one that's actually quite disconcerting. It bothers lots of people, particularly teachers, for reasons with which we could all empathize. Creative people regularly solve problems, as do intelligent people. Creative people fashion products, as do intelligent people. But creative people also raise new questions. They pose new issues. That's what we don't expect experts to do. I think that will change in the future, because anything algorithmic will be done by computers. It will be the raising of new questions that we'll be looking for.

Creators do things in a domain. That's the most interesting and controversial part of my definition. I don't believe people are creative or not creative in general any more than I believe that people are intelligent or not intelligent in general. People are intelligent in one or more intelligences. Even Leonardo [da Vinci] was intelligent in a few intelligences, not in all of them. People are creative in a domain. A domain is simply any structured activity in a society where we can rank people in terms of their expertise. An academic subject is a domain, an art form is a domain, running meetings is a domain, being a good gardener, zoo keeper, or actor is a domain. People are creative or not creative in a domain; they're not creative in general. Mozart was probably the most creative composer in history. But there's no reason to think he would have been particularly creative in other areas. In fact, I could give you some evidence that he wasn't. Similarly with Einstein: he played the fiddle but nobody ever accused him of being a creative fiddler.

Creativity is not just novelty; it requires ultimate acceptance. Anything you can do is novel. I could give the rest of my talk hopping up and down. That would clearly be novel. But if it wasn't ultimately accepted, it would just be stupid or entertaining. The acid test of creativity is: Are things in the future done differently in a domain? That really restricts creativity to a few people. It's true, only a few people change a domain profoundly, but lots of people change domains a little bit. Somebody once asked my friend Mihaly Csikszentmihalyi whether he was big C creative like the people that I study or little C creative, like the people who cook a meal a little bit differently. He said, "I'm middle C," which is, I think, what most of us can aspire to. We can't aspire to be an Einstein or a Virginia Woolf [a writer].

Csikszentmihalyi substituted for the familiar questions "Who is creative?" or "What is creativity?" the more provocative question of "Where is creativity?" Csikszentmihalyi and I maintain that creativity is not in the head. I could know what every neuron in your head did and every experience that you ever had, and I wouldn't have a clue as to whether you are creative or not. Why? Because creativity emerges from a dialectic among three different nodes. The vertices of this triangle: (1) individual talents; (2) domains or practices in a community, practices of expertise; and (3) fields, a new concept, which means the individuals or institutions that make judgments of originality and quality.

Let's concretize this. Say that you're all painters in New York. You're all trying to make a living as painters. It's hard. You're all individual talents. You've been instructed by the domain. You look at other paintings. You go to the museums. Maybe you go to art school. You're addressing the field. You're all making paintings. You hope they'll be noticed by a gallery owner, a critic, a prize giver, somebody with money to purchase paintings. Only one or two of you are even going to be noticed by the field. The rest of you will drive taxis or sell insurance which is, unfortunately, the plight of most artists in our society. But maybe two persons in every ten years will not only get the attention of the field, so they'll get a little notoriety, but they'll actually change the domain. Very few people get a chance to change domains, but when they do, the next generation of individual talents is instructed by a different set of practices, texts, and models.

Creativity is not in the head of the person. It's not in the domain. It's not in the field. It's an interaction. You can only understand creativity if you think about people doing activities in domains by which they've been instructed, addressing a field. A field judges what's worth paying attention to. A very few things that even are noticed eventually affect the domain for the future.

The acid test of creativity is very simple: Is the domain different? Now every one of you is thinking, *"Yea, but let's say the field is wrong."* There are only two answers to that. One answer is the answer of the guy at the filling station, "There's nothing I can do about it." The other is that "Fields can go on forever." Fields do change their minds, and new fields are created. When nobody paid any attention to Freud, he created a new field called "psychoanalysis." That field paid a lot of attention to Freud. The rediscovery or the new discovery of many women artists of the past occurs because new fields have been created to pay attention to that. But where Csikszentmihalyi and I draw the line is that judgment of creativity cannot be made independent of a field, a group of knowledgeable people.

Let's turn, finally, to the area of education. Educators are leaders, and leaders are educators. Well, that's an easy thing to say, and certainly it's a politically correct thing to say in this audience. But I actually mean it seriously for two primary reasons: One is more descriptive, one's more normative. Educators are in the business of transforming the mental representations of their students.

Otherwise, education is a waste of time. My objection to E. D. Hirsch, the literary scholar turned school reformer, is that I don't think he touches the mental representations, at least the way his ideas are usually implemented. But educators shouldn't be occupying space unless their goal is to change mental representations, and they can do that in many ways, including telling stories and, more important, by the kind of lives they lead. My one-sentence recipe for character education is to hang around parents and teachers who have good character.

The second and more normative connection between educators and leaders is that both educators and leaders face and confront the unschooled mind—leaders because they're dealing with heterogeneous groups, educators because the youngsters they are confronted with are unschooled, or there wouldn't be any need to educate them. The job of educators is to school unschooled minds, to transform the mental representations. It's very hard to change those mental representations. It's very hard to school the unschooled mind. So those are nontrivial connections between educators and leaders.

Three lessons

In my studies of creators and leaders, there are three lessons that one can draw. We can learn a lot from people like this. In fact, I think the demise of heroes in general or, to put it perhaps more tartly, substituting people who are not heroic but are treated as heroes for ones who truly are heroes is an abiding sin of our culture.

So I posed the question: What can we learn from extraordinary people?

Reflecting

My new book, *Extraordinary Minds,* expands on these three lessons. I call them reflecting, leveraging, and framing. Reflecting means spending a lot of time thinking about what you're doing and why and building in time for such reflection. These people all do a lot of reflecting. Even people like Churchill built time in their lives for reflecting. In fact, Churchill used to take baths all morning, and he wasn't just sleeping, he was thinking about things. "Not reflecting" is an abiding evil, or at least vice, of our time. Reflection is not a habit we develop in kids. I think our five-year-olds reflect as much as our sixteen-year-olds, and that is a troublesome state of affairs.

Leveraging

Leveraging is figuring out what you're good at, pushing it, and not worrying too much about what you're not good at. If you want to achieve something notable, figuring out your competitive advantage, what the niche is that you're better able to fill than other people, is a very adaptive thing to do. In fact, the word *adaptive* is probably appropriate because it's very Darwinian. Crying about spilled milk, things that you're not that good at, is not a very good use of time. You can for fun and profit try to get better at things you're not good at, but it's not really where your contributions are going to inhere. Extraordinary people spend a lot of time leveraging.

Framing

The third point, framing, grows out of the fact that people who are extraordinary have lots of bad things happen to them and have lots of failures. It comes with the territory. Many of us, including myself, when failing are prone either to give up or to ignore it. Both of these reactions are bad ideas. Framing means that when something hasn't gone well, recognize that it didn't go well but try to learn from it. Try to treat it as a positive experience, even as a moral lesson. Analyze it, dissect it, figure out what you might do differently.

Defeat is an opportunity

The most inspiring phrase I came across in my whole study was from Jean Monnet, the founder of the European Union. He said, "I regard every defeat as an opportunity." I've been literally stunned by how frequently that line appears in the study that I've done of extraordinary people. This turns out to be a real marker of extraordinary people. They convert apparent failures and defeats into learning opportunities. I also think it's a terribly important thing for parents, teachers, superintendents, and principals to do. When things don't go well—they need to recognize that in their own lives and then in the lives of the community for which they're responsible—they need to try to treat these setbacks as a learning experience. I love Esther Dyson's phrase "Make new mistakes." It's terrible to make no mistakes. It's good to make new mistakes and to learn from them.

Jean Monnet and Mahatma Gandhi—these are my heroes.

Morality

I want to talk about morality in general. When I study intelligence or creativity or leadership, I am not studying morality. I think any of these things can be used for good or for ill. Goethe had tremendous linguistic intelligence. So, unfortunately, did Joseph Goebbels. They used it for very different ends. Many politicians have wonderful interpersonal intelligence. They can use it to foment hatred, to manipulate people, or to try to do good. It's the same with creativity. Many of the most awful people in the world are very creative, and many people like Malcolm X can go either way with their creativity. It's the same with educators. Probably more education is done in America nowadays by talk show hosts than by many classroom teachers, and yet I certainly wouldn't defend what most talk show hosts are doing.

A lot of people say, "Howard, why do you study Margaret Thatcher when she's such an awful person?" I don't happen to think that Margaret Thatcher is an awful person, but I would study her even if I did think she was if I thought we could learn from her.

I think it's a big mistake in research and analysis to only study the good guys, to only study the people whom you like. There's a lot to be learned from people whom you don't admire or, in the case of Margaret Thatcher (in my case), whom you're ambivalent about.

Heroes

This is not to say, however, that I don't have people whom I admire. As noted, I admire tremendously Jean Monnet and Mahatma Gandhi because they tried to be inclusionary. They recognized the unschooled mind and tried to move it in ways which they thought were productive. I call them leaders across national boundaries.

Monnet started as a Frenchman, but he eventually sought to unite all of Europe and effect an Atlantic alliance. His model is now being copied in many regions of the world.

Gandhi was an Indian, but he spent half of his life in South Africa. His influence is truly global. Gandhi was more of a religious figure than Monnet. Gandhi really went back to human fundamentals and said, "We don't have to disagree by killing each other, we can do so in other ways and people can be strengthened by the disagreement. It's not a zero sum game." Gandhi studied all the world's religions. Moreover, he worked out a kind of an algebra of nonviolent resistance which was much more than a slogan, it was really a new way of going about doing these things. He created a complicated story and he embodied it.

Monnet and Gandhi are heroes of mine not only because I like their stories and I like their lives, they are heroes because they began with the unschooled mind, but they were not content to end there.

Hitler began with the unschooled mind and pandered to it. In fact, he probably brought it down a few notches. He went from the five-year-old mind to the two- or three-year-old mind.

To me the challenge is to go beyond the five-year-old mind and to convey more complicated notions about the world, about human beings and nations, than the ideas we first acquire when we are five.

I don't consider myself devoid of a moral sensibility, and my work now is in the area of ethics. But as an analyst, I want to make a very sharp distinction between the way I would like things to be and trying to understand the phenomenon. Whether we're dealing with intelligence or creativity or leadership, it's very salutary to remember that all of these things can be used both ways. They have to be related to a community and to a set of values before we can make judgments about the ways in which they are used.

Max De Pree
Chairman Emeritus
Herman Miller, Inc.
Holland, Michigan

During his forty years with Herman Miller, Inc., Max De Pree served in various management roles, the last eight as Chief Executive Officer.

Mr. De Pree began his college studies at Wheaton College, studied at various universities while in the service during World War II, which included eighteen months in the European Theatre of Operations, and received his B.A. from Hope College.

Mr. De Pree serves on the Board of Trustees of Fuller Theological Seminary and the Advisory Board of the Peter F. Drucker Foundation.

He is the author of *Leadership Is an Art, Leadershp Jazz, Dear Zoe,* and *Leading Without Power.*

In 1997, Mr. De Pree received the Lifetime Achievement Award from the Business Enterprise Trust.

Max De Pree

Chapter 2

What's a Movement?

Over the years, I have become increasingly aware of a singular, qualitative difference among organizations. Most organizations are, well, just organizations, collections of people and assets that serve a purpose. Sometimes they thrive, sometimes they don't. They meet certain needs and have a certain legitimacy in society.

Then there are other exceptional organizations that we can more precisely call movements. Beth Israel Hospital in Boston (the first hospital in the United States to publish a declaration of patient rights and to incorporate employee and patient ideas into its operations), Willow Creek Community Church west of Chicago (which reaches out into the unchurched culture rather than expecting all people to reach out to the church), InterVarsity Christian Fellowship in Madison, Wisconsin (a pioneer in Christian ministries in higher education, business, and ethnic cultures), and Apple Computer in its formative years—movements like these dot the organizational landscape and serve as models of energy and devotion to a compelling cause. They illustrate new ways of working together. They set standards of effective function and enlightened contribution. They give us a picture of what a place of realized potential can be.

Recognizing a movement

A movement is a collective state of mind, a public and common understanding that the future can be created, not simply

The lecture by Max De Pree was based on chapter two of his book *Leading Without Power,* published by Jossey-Bass, San Francisco, Calif., 1997. Chapter two, with minor changes, is reprinted by permission of Jossey-Bass.

experienced or endured. Many of us never have the good fortune to belong to such a group, where becoming is a way of living and working together.

Movements are easier to recognize from the inside. There is a harmony in relationships and a constructive conflict of ideas. There is a palpable unity as the people there implement their vision. There is a rhythm of innovation and renewal. There's a sense of urgency—movements are never casual. Alongside the normal tensions of organized life, there is a high level of trust.

When I first began to date the girl who later married me, I had to deal with an unexpected phenomenon. I was being introduced into a kissing family. Now it wasn't that I didn't love my own sisters and aunts, but my family just wasn't as demonstrative as Esther's. I had several dates with Esther before I dared ask for a kiss. But Esther's five aunts didn't have any timidity; they didn't believe in shaking hands. Each new boyfriend at the family reunion was welcomed immediately with hugs and kisses.

Like kissing families, movements have their distinguishing marks. In movements, people tell stories about giants and about failures. They tell stories about relationships and surprises. They tell stories as a way of teaching. They tell stories as a way of preserving and remembering the past. Movements thrive on their stories. We are defined by our stories, which form us and make us vital and give us hope. Stories teach and preserve traditions and practices and policies and values. I don't know many people who prefer a manual to a myth. Our fidelity to our stories, like fidelity to choices, shapes our characters and in so doing shapes the movements of which we are a part. Stories play a key role in our movements because they are the vehicles through which we expose and, therefore, greatly reduce the temptation to impose.

Requirements of a movement

Can an organization intentionally shape itself into a movement? It certainly seems reasonable that we can discuss a variety of requirements that movements seem to meet.

Spirit-lifting leadership

One of the first things required in movements is spirit-lifting leadership, leadership that enables, enriches, holds the organization accountable, and in the end lets go.

Competence

Also high on the list of requirements is competence. I would expect a movement to be highly participatory, but I would also expect people there to realize that participation and representation are no substitutes for simple competence. Character cannot replace competence. When I think about competence, I mean competence in relationships as well as technical competence, for poor relationships sabotage even the most competent persons. Success in our jobs requires technical competence; success as human beings requires competence in relationships.

Creativity

A movement requires a high sense of creativity. In some places of realized potential, creativity becomes a moral issue: it is the means through which we protect the human environment. In others it becomes a process of discovery to bring about necessary change. Some of the resulting transitions are actually things the organization can't really afford at the time, but the dangers of equivocation are clear. The transitions will be designed and implemented without fear of either the creative person or the change she brings about.

I remember so well the time in Herman Miller's history when we didn't have money to buy the tool for Charles Eames's first molded fiberglass chair. We all knew that producing the chair was the right thing to do, but how were we going to pay for the tool? Our national sales manager volunteered to loan the company the money—a risky and creative thing for him to do. We bought the tool, and the chair was a great success. Within a short time we managed to repay the money. Thanks to Jim Eppinger, the sales manager, our organization had passed a crucial transition.

Commitment

One of the beauties of a movement is the clear commitment

to substance over bureaucracy. Superficial and trivial activities give way to a serious concern for content and substance, priorities and discipline. Movements tend to create a wonderful breadth of mind in the people involved, whether the group focuses on human relations or engineering or financial affairs. There arises from the concern for true substance a real thread of optimism and openness about life.

Respect

A movement is almost always a civil place, where people respect each other and work for a common good—where they understand that good manners, civil language, and decorum are assets. People respect the constructive mystery of simplicity, fidelity, clarity, and beauty. They are grateful for the contribution of others to their lives and work—even if sometimes they don't quite see how it happens.

When Allan Houser, the great Native American sculptor, was seventy-eight years old, he continued to start each day with a rigorous exercise routine. He knew that if he had no strength in his body, he would not be able to execute the creativity in his heart. One of the wonderful facets of a movement is the existence of disciplined routines in the midst of freedom.

Signs of trouble

Of course, we have to consider that movements tend to deteriorate into mere organizations. Some of the signs: We begin to make trade-offs. We begin to prefer comfort to ambiguity. We look for control rather than challenge (it's always easier to deal with commodities than uniqueness). We begin to trust job assignments rather than respecting individual gifts.

I know a young man who has enormous gifts in writing and in music. He's a performer and composer; he's been a filmmaker and writer. He had been plugging away for a number of years in the purchasing department of a large corporation and suddenly found himself, for no reason at all, terminated in a misguided cost-saving cutback. The detour of unemployment soon led him to a new job in a much smaller company doing exactly what his gifts enable him to do best. Not only does he have a bright new life but his employer has gained an important competitive advantage. His former employers to this day have no idea what they missed—all because they looked too much at assignments and too little at the gifts of persons.

Trouble often comes to movements when we change our common stories—out of embarrassment or because we can't believe or accept them or because the stories suddenly seem naive. New volunteers come with new visions and often, without realizing it, change history so that the new organization can move like the old. Rewriting history is a risky business. In movements, stories give life; in organizations, stories manipulate people.

Movements suffer when common sense is hailed as innovation, when job descriptions replace expectations, when risky choices become diluted into no-risk decisions, when poets are terminated and bureaucrats promoted, when finishing a project—no matter how routine or unremarkable—is celebrated as an achievement. Movements ache when leaders lose their sense of dependence on the often quiet but indispensable folks who keep things going so remarkably well, day in and day out.

Movements degrade when rules dominate decision-making. Some years ago, our family was living in London, where I was working at the time. Both miniskirts and pantsuits were in vogue. My wife had recently purchased a pantsuit with a long jacket. We had guests from the States in our party of seven or eight as we headed for Simpson's in the Strand, whose reputation for a good old English dinner of roast beef is still well known. The maître d' took one look at Esther in her new pantsuit, called me off to one side, and informed me that Simpson's did not allow women to wear trousers to dinner. I asked him quietly if Esther would be permitted to wear only her long jacket as a minidress. He immediately agreed to that. Esther, however, felt differently and had no intention of taking off her trousers. The maître d' held his ground, and off we went to another restaurant. We have never been back to Simpson's, the restaurant that had for my family, in that moment of truth, become a mere organization.

Finally, and maybe most important, movements suffer when leaders are unable or unwilling to hold the group accountable. Only leaders are able to hold an entire group accountable to itself and to others. If they don't, the movement will become just another organization, having lost its standing in a spirit-quenching moment. When I consider the reasons to work for a movement, it helps to remember this ineluctable fact of life: we are sentenced to live with who we become.

Character
and Morals

Dr. Cornelius Plantinga, Jr.
Dean of the Chapel
Calvin College
Grand Rapids, Michigan

Dr. Cornelius Plantinga, Dean of the Chapel at Calvin College, is a graduate of Calvin College and Calvin Theological Seminary. He also attended Yale University and received a Ph.D. degree from Princeton Theological Seminary.

He is the author of numerous essays and four books, including *Not the Way It's Supposed to Be: A Breviary of Sin*, which won the Christianity Today Book of the Year Award in 1996.

He served as concertmaster of the Grand Rapids Symphony Orchestra from 1968–70.

Cornelius Plantinga, Jr.

Chapter 3

Character Matters I:
Contours of Character

Let's start by thinking about Jimmy Stewart. After he died last month, the major news magazines couldn't decide which they liked better—Stewart or his movies. There have been all those terrific movies, of course, and Stewart played a lot of very different characters in them. He wasn't always the Aw Shucks guy next door who would "gosh" and "golly" his way into the heart of every freedom-loving American. Some of his characters were dark—full of obsession, or of a sense of betrayal, or of anguish. Jimmy Stewart was an actor of considerable range and achievement, but what the news accounts really wanted to talk about last month was not the actor, but the man himself.

Who was Jimmy Stewart? Well, he was the generous and long-lasting husband of Gloria Stewart, married to her for 45 years; he was funny and self-deprecating; he was good-willed and good-humored. He was so decent a man—so modest and civil and gracious—that when he died *Time* magazine said: "A beloved man is dead, and we mourn, for our loss at least as much as his." *Newsweek* said that Stewart made us nostalgic for a time "before self-promotion came into vogue, [a time] when a man still blushed when good things were said about him," a time "in which a movie star might also be a gentleman."

Jimmy Stewart in life and in death was at least as much admired for his character as for his acting, and this fact leads me into my topic for today and tomorrow.

Good character and evidence we are losing it

As you know, in the last four or five years lots of people in this country have been talking about character, and they have almost always talked about it as a corrective. Why? Where do we need correcting?

The usual answer is that we have become uncivil people. It's not just that we don't vote. It's not just that volunteer agencies need more volunteers. It's not that we try to avoid our taxes. After all, as the saying goes, tax evasion is criminal, but tax avoidance is American.

No, we are uncivil in a much larger and more serious sense.

How so?

You know the litany as well as I do. I'm speaking of the litany of ills that has shown up in scores of articles in the last decade. Our families break down too often. We have built up a whole culture of divorce, as Barbara Dafoe Whitehead has recently written (*The Divorce Culture,* Knopf, 1997). We make kids, but we don't care for them. We lie to each other. We sue each other a lot. We shoot at each other much oftener than people in other countries do. Our students cheat on tests and regard cheating as normal. Our eleven-year-olds do an Internet search for death metal bands and come up with 120 Web sites, most with lyrics—if lyrics is not too lyrical a word—about the glories of necrophilia and of other ways to enjoy a corpse.

An uncivil people

We are uncivil people in the large sense of that word—i.e., we vandalize our own society. We act against the big structures that hold society together. But we are also uncivil in the narrower sense of that word. I mean that we have become ungenerous to each other—ungracious, discourteous, plain rude—so that it's time for reformation in the land.

You hear and read of such incivility all the time: students who curse teachers; airline passengers who bump flight attendants around; drivers who cut people off and then flip them off, just to show who's king of the road. What has gotten a lot of folks alarmed is not merely that people sometimes behave badly, which they have done for a very long time, but that they also have a certain attitude about it. The attitude sometimes has a kind of casual nihilism in it, and nothing illustrates this attitude better than a story that my friend and teacher Lewis Smedes tells in one of his books.

Lew's wife, Doris, was waiting in line at a self-service gas station one day, fourth in line for a diesel pump that could be gotten at from either side of the island. After the three cars ahead of her had finished, she pulled up to the pump, got out of the car, and briefly turned her back to remove the cap to her tank. Then she turned to reach for the nozzle. Meanwhile, "a new station wagon that was full of family splashed up" on the other side of the pump, and the driver "sprang out of the front seat, grabbed the nozzle just as Doris reached for it, and then spun the cap off his own tank and began to whistle as he filled his tank with diesel fuel."

Doris was momentarily stunned by this remarkable turn of events, but then she began to speak to the other driver. "I think you saw that I was waiting in line for this pump before you got here," she said.

"That makes no difference to me," said the other driver.

"Well," said Doris, "I think that what you are doing is contemptible."

"But I don't give a damn what you think," said the guy.

Doris tried once more: "Your children are watching," she said. "Don't you care what they think?"

"Look, lady," the other driver said, "I told you I don't care what *you* think."

Well, if this is the way life goes in America's gas stations, I suppose it's no wonder that we have heavy weather in some of our schoolrooms. What's remarkable here, of course, is not just this man's cutting in line, which is bad enough. Or his lack of remorse, though that's worse. What's truly unsettling about this man's behavior is his breezy indifference both to what he had done and to what people would inevitably think of it.

This man has five of his senses, but not the sixth. He seems to lack a *moral* sense. In addition, he lacks what the Declaration of Independence calls "a decent respect for the opinions of mankind."

A guy like this makes one long for the return of good old-fashioned hypocrisy. A hypocrite at least pretends to be good. A hypocrite has some standards—the same ones as the rest of us. We know he has these standards because he pretends to meet them. Hypocrisy has had a bad name, William Raspberry said in one of his commencement speeches, "but that doesn't bother me. What bothers me is that we have stopped the actual *practice* of hypocrisy. Once upon a time people upheld the standards even as they broke them. Once upon a time people would say to themselves, 'You know, what I'm doing is wrong, so I must not do it too often, I must pretend not to do it at all, and above all I must take care not to get caught at it.'" Once upon a time people understood La Rochefoucauld's maxim, namely, that "Hypocrisy is the homage that vice pays to virtue."

And so once upon a time people would pretend and defend and rationalize and explain away. Now they say, "Just do it." Now they say, "If it feels good, do it." Now, at the gas pump, people say, "Lady, I really don't give a damn."

We have talked for decades about crime, especially about violent crime. We have deplored assault and abuse and rape and all the hate crimes, not to mention the hundreds of ingenious frauds that make life precarious and expensive. In short, we have deplored law-breaking just as we should. But you notice that there's no law against what the guy in the gas station did. There's no law against what he said. There's no law against what he taught his children that day as they sat in their station wagon and watched their daddy one-up a strange lady. God has laws against this kind of thing, but the government doesn't.

What I'm saying is that for human life to be tolerable together, let alone for it to flourish, we need more than lots of laws and lots of freedom. We need something else. We need citizens of good character who will carry on where the law leaves off—carry on in the same trajectory of fairness, decency, goodwill, and accountability. (I sometimes think we also ought to have small bands of benevolent vigilantes who would do things like round up the guy in the station wagon and make him watch a Jimmy Stewart film festival and maybe write a ten-page report on *Mr. Smith Goes to Washington*.)

In a good society good character will generate good law, but also go way beyond it. A lot of people in a lot of places these days have been noticing this. Everybody's talking about character and about our need to reform it. You might think this is merely routine. You might think that every so often when things get bad enough, people automatically start to grump and complain and demand programs of character reform right in the same breath that they demand tax and campaign reform.

Maybe so and maybe not. Maybe some of the recent renewal of interest in character comes from real alarm at the real novelty of the kind of macho indifference we see in people like the guy at the gas station.

In either case, there's no doubt we are right in the middle of a back-to-character movement. Sometimes people in the movement talk about virtue, or the virtues, or the cardinal virtues, and that's understandable enough since morally good character is one in which you can spot a fine sampling of such human virtues as generosity, courage, and a hunger for justice. Try thinking of it like this: If virtues are pieces of good fruit, then good character is at least a medium-sized fruit basket. A good-character fruit basket might not have all the kinds of fruit there are, but it will definitely have some of the basic ones such as compassion, fairness, self-control, and prudence. It will also have a good sampling of many others, such as patience, gratitude, generosity, and a willingness to pick up after oneself.

The back-to-character movement

Some of the people who talk about character do so by publishing books. What we've had in the past four years or so is a flurry of published works that seek to improve our character by presenting virtues and encouraging us to acquire them. Hence Bill Bennett's *The Book of Virtues* (1993), which got praised and damned by reviewers, but mostly praised, and which, in any case, stayed on the *New York Times'* bestseller list for many, many months. Bennett has

since followed up with a couple of other character books, and he's
not the only national figure who has been playing this theme.

There's also Stephen Carter, the Yale Law School professor
who has written on affirmative action and on the culture of disbe-
lief. Stephen Carter has recently published a fine book on integ-
rity. Moreover, both Dan Quayle and Hilary Rodham Clinton published books last year (quite different ones) on proper child-rearing
and on the teaching of morality to children.

While we're in the publishing department I might mention
Herbert Kohl and Colin Greer's book *A Call to Character,* which
includes proverbs and stories just as Bennett's books do, but which
sets the moral compass in a little different direction. According to
Wray Herbert, who comments on the difference, Bennett wants
people to learn courage and valor from William Tell and Henry V,
while Kohl and Greer want people to learn playfulness, balance,
and irony from Arnold Lobel's Frog and Toad.

Either way, character is back. Both the President and the First
Lady have been speaking quite often of personal responsibility as
part of what defines new Democrats. Since 1994, the President
has sponsored joint meetings between Congress and the White
House in which the main topic is character-building. The White
House has also been hosting conferences on good character and on
how government can inspire all the rest of us to build it. In 1994
the U.S. Senate created a new caucus entitled Character Counts
which in turn proposed a resolution to the full Senate to declare a
national week of recognition that "character counts." Well, the Senate
could hardly deny that character counts, so it declared that during
the week of October 16–22 of that year character would *really* count.

Programs of these kinds have naturally gotten the wags and
cynics to wonder whether government is necessarily the first place
we want to go for lessons in virtue. (I'm reminded of those rare
times when a government agency turns for help to the underworld
in order to apprehend a criminal on the principle that it takes a
thief to catch a thief, and then all the skeptics complain that the
agency could just as easily have saved the taxpayers' money by
handling this assignment with in-house staff.) I guess that's America.

But remember William Raspberry's lesson: We shouldn't let violations of the standards erase the standards. We shouldn't let violations of the standards make us cynical. Cynicism about national life and politics is just as unhelpful as anything the cynics charge the politicians with. In any case, hypocrisy beats indifference. "If preaching standards that we know will be violated—if preaching standards that we know will be violated even by those of us who preach them—if that constitutes hypocrisy," says William Raspberry, "then let's hear it for hypocrisy."

Do we all understand his point? It's bad to be a hypocrite. But it's worse—much worse—to be the guy at the gas pump.

Which reminds us that good people find incivility not just annoying, but alarming, and especially when it comes packaged with moral indifference.

The result is that a lot of people have welcomed and joined the back-to-character movement. Book publishers have gotten into it. Government agencies have gotten into it. I'm sure I don't have to tell you distinguished educators from around the land that many of the nation's schools have joined the movement. Indeed, some of the nation's schools—including some of yours, I'm sure—never left the movement.

In fact, character education is as old as education itself. For centuries, educators have used stories, modeling, and various forms of discipline, including praise and reproach, in an attempt to instill virtue and suppress vice in their students. For centuries, educators have assumed that character education is one of the bonds between the generations, one of the supports of civil society, and one of the surest signs of respect for each other. After all, as Gilbert Meilaender put it, taking seriously the development of good character in young persons is simply one of the most obvious ways of taking *them* seriously.

As a way of taking students seriously, the most recent character education movements in the nation's public schools go beyond the older values clarification and Kohlbergian cognitive analysis programs and actually try to inculcate virtue. Local and state boards of education adopt statements and policies encouraging schools to integrate character education into their established curricula, and then schools have a go at it.

The state of Michigan, for instance, adopted a policy on character nine months ago which states that "principles such as respect, responsibility, caring, trustworthiness, justice, civic virtue, and citizenship determine the character of our people and the tenor of the society in which we live.... these principles transcend religious belief and are the foundation for an orderly and civil society." The statement then goes on to offer a description of character education, a rationale for it, and a list of resources to support it.

Nationally, as I've been discovering, a number of coalitions that center on character education have sprung up within the last few years. The Character Education Partnership, for example, comprises more than fifty organizations and helps them talk together in order to strengthen the curricula and programming which each develops. Many of these agencies, such as The Center for the Fourth and Fifth R's run by Thomas Lickona of SUNY Cortland, and The Center for the Advancement of Ethics and Character directed by Kevin Ryan of Boston University, host conferences, publish books and newsletters, and train teachers, administrators, and community leaders. The CHARACTER COUNTS! program generated out of the Josephson Institute of Ethics (Marina del Rey, California) has gotten more than one hundred schools and public-service agencies nationwide to observe the third week of October as Character Counts Week. Their idea is to affirm and celebrate good character through the use of discussion forums, parades, and community celebrations. The idea is to stir up whole communities—not just schools—to good works in this area.

Why do we need stirring up? What has gone wrong? According to a fairly typical cultural analysis, the cultural revolution of the '60s and '70s—whatever its virtues, and there were some—has brought us the characteristic sins of the '80s and '90s, namely, impatience, flight from accountability, and the deifying of the self and its choices. It has brought us people like the guy in the gas station.

Given these unhappinesses, we can easily recognize some of

the characteristic assumptions that often accompany them—namely, that morality is simply a matter of personal taste, that rights are more important than responsibilities, that liberty can be enjoyed without virtue, that self-reproach is unnecessary and maybe irrelevant, that it is more satisfying to be envied than respected, and that life is for consuming and especially for consuming entertainment products.

It's important to see that it's not just social conservatives who have been ringing the alarms lately. Dan Quayle thought that the famous *Murphy Brown* episode was distorted, and he took a lot of heat for it. But some major media, including *Newsweek* and *The Atlantic Monthly*, thought the matter over for a while, decided Dan Quayle was right, and said so. Moreover, the people who worry about materialism in this country, about our consumer mentality and the way we have turned buying into a sacrament, are certainly not just political or social conservatives. There's a huge middle group of concerned people who yearn for good character, who believe that it has been eroding, and who think it's time to try to rebuild it. They think this merely because they are people who would like to live in a well-ordered society that flourishes in the area that lies between personal freedom and the prohibitions of law—an area made civil by people who are respectful, disciplined, and good-willed.

Think of this for a moment: Colin Powell could get elected from any political party he chose. He has the sort of character that people who are otherwise very different from each other combine to want. What we want is virtue. What we want is character that includes a good blend of the soft virtues such as love, kindness, and compassion, and the hard virtues that put spine in our character—such virtues as justice, courage, and self-control. What we want, in short, is for people to be good. I know that to a certain sort of moral skeptic, this program sounds quaint. To me and maybe to some of you and certainly to lots of concerned folk, it sounds like the sober truth. We need to be and to become good people and we need to teach our students, our children, and our grandchildren to become so.

Of course, alert people in every age have fretted over the corruption of culture, and in every age they have been right to do so. The reason is clear, I believe: Morally speaking, it's a lot easier to wreck something than to build it. It's a lot easier to pollute than to clean up pollution. Corruption of what's good is the way things tend to go. Appoint a police force to keep order, and certain members of it will become tyrants who bully their way around people's neighborhoods. Hook people up to the Internet and you will extend the range not only of educators and physicians but also of crooks and pedophiles. Get people to worship God and pretty soon we who are religious start using religion to bend other people to our agenda. It happens all the time. And when it does, it's shameful.

So every time is the right time for character reformation. Every time is the right time for respect and responsibility (which are Lickona's fourth and fifth R's). One reason is that public good is hard to achieve and hard to maintain. I remember thinking in 1964 as an idealistic 18-year-old that when Lyndon Johnson signed the Civil Rights Bill, we Americans had made it. I remember thinking: "This is it. Racism has been licked. The President has just made it illegal. Now we can forget about that problem and turn toward others."

Who foresaw the David Duke phenomenon at that time? Who foresaw white backlash and the assassination of Martin Luther King, Jr., and affirmative-action debates? The sad truth is that the public good is precarious. One of the reasons is that the people who are in favor of it backslide a lot.

Every time is the right time for character reform.

What is character?

But what are we are talking about when we talk about character?

For the purposes of these speeches, when I talk about character I'm talking about moral character—the part of who we are that could be called loving or hateful, envious or grateful, resentful or forgiving, kind or cruel. I'm not talking about temperament. Some

people are seemingly born irritable and jumpy, and some are seemingly born sunny-side up. Every parent knows this. People have
different temperaments and they seem to have them from the start.
But temperament isn't the same thing as character. Morally speaking, temperament is by itself neither here nor there. Temperament
is only a part of the raw material from which character is made.
Where character is concerned, everything depends on what we do
about our temperament.

Something similar should be said of personality. Some folk
are extroverted to the point of being flashy; some are so introverted
that they want to apologize for taking up space on the planet.
Some people are easily amused; others have a sense of humor that
lies so far below the surface that you have to fish for it. Where
personality is concerned, people are noisy or quiet, social or reclu-
sive, deliberate or impulsive, quick or ponderous. None of this is,
by itself, a feature of moral character, though, again, all of it is raw
material for our character. For example, a person whose noisiness
prevents others from sleeping or thinking, and who knows this and
yet makes no effort to control her noisiness, has a character flaw in
addition to a personality trait. On the other hand, a person who
strives to control her noisiness out of consideration for others has a
character virtue. And this is true even when she doesn't succeed,
for she is considerate enough to try.

Temperament and personality traits—and we could add in all
the other inherited and environmental influences that push and
pull us in a hundred ways that we aren't even aware of—are the
raw material of moral character. The finished product, the actual
moral face that we show to the world, depends on what we do with
our raw material. There's a reason why Colin Powell, for example,
answers questions in the way that he does. There's a reason why he
speaks of his wife and her battles with depression in the way that
he does. To take just one obvious reason: Colin Powell has spent
years and years learning self-discipline. You can't be a good soldier,
or a good spouse, or even an honest conversation partner in a press
conference without it. Colin Powell has it. He's got what the old
philosophers called temperance—the ability to tame and discipline

one's passions. Passions are part of our raw material; General Powell's character is the finished product that combines passion and discipline.

A sample virtue: compassion

So what is this finished product that people are talking about so much these days? Good character, I said earlier, is a fruit basket of virtues. A person of good character will have some combination of such virtues as temperance, courage, compassion, and generosity. But what is a virtue?

A virtue is a good disposition. It's an acquirable tendency of a certain sort. It's a tendency to think, feel, speak, and act along a certain very good line.

Let's take compassion as an example. Almost every character reformation program in the country lists compassion as one of its core virtues. It's a consensus winner in the character derby.

To characterize compassion, let's recall the film *The Elephant Man*. This film tells the story of an Englishman who is unspeakably ugly. He's so ugly he has to wrap his face so that he won't scare children and stop traffic. For a while a drunk gets hold of him, cages him, and charges admission for private viewings. Later, a physician takes him in and in wonderful ways rebuilds his dignity. At one point the Elephant Man tries to say what such kind treatment has meant to him. And so he opens the voice hole in his face and begins to rasp out of it: "I now feel joy," he says, "because I know I am loved." Another time, he recites part of the Twenty-Third Psalm. The twisted lips say, "Surely goodness and mercy shall follow me all the days of my life and I shall dwell in the house of the Lord forever."

As the film progresses, the Elephant Man faces jokes and cackles and various humiliations forced on him by crude people. These things are painful to witness. But when you witness them, something happens. What happens is that as you watch the Elephant Man get abused, you move over to his side. Emotionally you stand next to him. Like the caring physician, you want to shield the Elephant Man. You want to minister to him. You identify with this ugly human being so that his joys become your joys, his enemies your enemies. His dignity makes you proud. Above all, you feel his pain and you want to protect and nurture him.

You feel compassion.

Hard joy and easy misery

Compassion is an important emotion and unless we have been coarsened by war or daytime television, we feel it every so often. You speak with a student who has been used up and thrown away by her careless boyfriend, as if she were disposable tissue. When she describes her sense of humiliation—almost of horror—at the way she has been handled, you commiserate. You feel mixed anger and pity. Or you view a telecast of children in Romania whose dislocation is so great that they have become hookers at age nine. You move a little way inside their situation and note once more that children are incorrigibly hopeful creatures: their lives may be wrecked, but they cling to every thread of promise and even of rumor. The mixture of wreckage and hope pulls at you. You commiserate, you compassionate (to use a good old English word). Your innards feel as if somebody is pulling the drawstrings tight.

Or imagine a lighter scenario. Your timid son is performing for the first time in his piano teacher's studio recital in front of all the other students and parents. His prepared piece is "March of the Candy Soldiers," and for thirty bars or so he plays it pretty well. But then some of the soldiers start to lose their way, and your son panics, and the performance dissolves into a muddle of dissonances and false starts. Finally your son turns red, gets up, and walks miserably back to his chair at your side. You pity. You commiserate. You feel compassion clear down to your viscera.

What do we mean when we say you have the virtue of compassion? As my friend Calvin Van Reken likes to put it, we mean you have a light trigger, a hair trigger for generating the empathetic pity that identifies with a suffering person. You are readily disposed to suffer with the suffering. You have a soft heart. In the presence of suffering you quite soon do, I'll say, five things:

(1) You perceive the suffering. That's a big thing right there,

of course. Suffering is easy to miss if you don't want to see it. The suffering of others is easy to miss if you are already stuffed with yourself. But if you are compassionate, you will notice the suffering of others.

(2) You empathize with the sufferer. I mean you identify with the sufferer. You see something of yourself in her. In his book *Spirituality and Human Emotion,* Robert C. Roberts ponders the empathy dimension of compassion. He calls it an "I, too" phenomenon.

Here's the idea: Suppose you are an empathetic person. When you see someone suffer, you instinctively resonate in some way that, if stated, would come to something like this: "I, too, am susceptible to suffering."

When you note somebody's laziness, you say, "I, too, am weak and deficient in many ways." When you approach the bed of a dying person, you feel empathetic pangs of mortality, and you say, "I, too, will die."

The empathy in compassion is an "I, too" phenomenon. When you behold a sinner—someone detected in a sleazy, boring, garden-variety sin, or somebody detected in a big, juicy, scandalous sin—you do not rub your hands together and gloat over this person's misery or save it for happy-hour gossip with your friends. Surely you do not take comfort from it. No, as an empathetic person, you say to yourself, "I, too, am a sinner, badly in need of forgiveness." And you are able to weep with those who weep.

The point is (3) that you feel sorrow over another's suffering. Not gladness, not indifference, not annoyance, but sorrow.

And (4) you want to relieve it. That's your disposition. If you so much as anticipate somebody's suffering (the way, for example, parents anticipate a child's response to a necessary but painful medical procedure) you will want to relieve this suffering every way you can.

(5) And then you will follow through, if possible, and actually protect or relieve the sufferer.

The upshot is that a compassionate person is one who in the presence of distress readily displays traits (1) through (5). That's her disposition. That's the way she leans. That's who she is.

It's important to see, I believe, that in order to have good character, we need to have more than one virtue and more than one kind of virtue. We need some hard virtues along with some soft ones. We've got to have more than one sort of fruit in the basket.

It's therefore important to insist that compassion does not trump justice or relativize all moral judgment. A compassionate person will defer judgment while attending to more urgent matters and will often temper justice. But she will still let justice roll down like mighty waters right along with the streams of compassion.

Remember that ranking Nazis used to weep over Wagnerian operas. They had sentimentality, but not compassion. Or, perhaps closer to the truth, they had compassion, but it was selective because it was unaccompanied by justice. The virtue of justice is the disposition to give people what is due to them, to give them what they have coming, and to do this both distributively and retributively. As we all know, the Nazi failure to give people due respect and equal protection of the law, and the Nazi fondness for punishing people who didn't deserve to be punished—these injustices have become a twentieth century emblem of evil.

Compassion without justice is sentimental. And justice without compassion is mechanical. Each needs the other. We need more than one kind of fruit in our basket.

We can now notice something else. Along with our compassion we need not only justice; we also need temperance. We need to be able to discipline our feelings of compassion so that they won't paralyze us. Hand-wringing won't get the job done. Compassion is a terrific motive, but without discipline it will burn a person out.

If I'm in a lot of physical distress because I need a coronary artery bypass operation, and if I should be so happily situated as to have a superb surgeon—Dr. Tomatis, for example—I will want him to temper whatever feelings of compassion he has. To put it clearly, if I'm going to have surgery in the morning, I do not want Dr. Tomatis to stay up all night feeling compassionate. I want him to sleep like a baby and then get up in the morning feeling pretty brisk. I want him to be humane and businesslike at the same time.

Good character is like good government: It's got a system of checks and balances going in it. And so, along with compassion and justice we need temperance. We also need the virtue of prudence. Prudence is practical wisdom. Prudence tells us how to apply the other virtues in practical situations. For example, suppose you are confronted with a distressed person. Compassion disposes you to relieve his distress. But compassion all by itself doesn't tell you how. It doesn't dictate one strategy rather than another. For that you need prudence. You need good judgment. Does the sufferer need to go to work or to bed? Should he sue or repent? Would you serve him best by giving him money, or a reprimand, or a few kind words, or what?

People wonder about this kind of thing all the time. And they may attempt to apply their compassion differently on different occasions, depending on their history with the sufferer. For example, the theory of tough love says that eventually we may get to a place in our relationship with one of our own children that the most compassionate thing we can do for him is to change the locks on the family house.

And, of course, we do have, and must have, the same debate nationally and politically. A lot of the current debate about the new welfare laws is about prudence. Most people of good will believe that it is both compassionate and just to help the poor. But what's the most prudent way to do it? Suppose that what a jobless person needs is not just a job offer, and not just job-training, but also character-training. Where's that going to come from?

In the *Wall Street Journal* a few years ago (August 16, 1995) Richard Barclay wrote a piece about this problem. I present it not because I have any answer to the problem Barclay raises but because I do not and because I think it's the sort of problem prudent people will be thoughtful about. The problem speaks directly to the intersection of personal character, business life, and public policy.

Richard Barclay is vice president of a Riverside, California, telephone remanufacturing company, and he has interviewed hundreds of people for jobs that start just above minimum wage and go up from there. The problem he describes—one a lot of people are thinking about in the advent of changed welfare laws—is that some people are mysteriously unemployable.

Some people, says Barclay, can't work. "They are physically competent. They are mentally competent. But they literally cannot work. They look normal, they sound normal, they are trainable, and they say they want to have a job. But they confuse wanting money with wanting to work—which for some weird reason they just can't do. They simply can't be on time. They simply can't work quickly. They simply can't follow instructions. It's just the way they are."

So, says Barclay, here's a problem. You want to employ these folks. You try to employ these folks. But something gets in the way. And what's in the way is not what a businessperson necessarily feels competent to address.

Barclay says, "For the lower-echelon, unskilled positions, companies don't need 'trained' applicants so much as they need people of character. I can train a person to disassemble a phone," he says, "but I cannot train her not to get a bad attitude when she's expected to show up for work every day when the rest of us are there."

Here we can see that different clusters of virtues seem to be necessary for different parts of human life. Barclay's job applicants need some combination of industriousness, punctuality, teachableness, and general reliability. Without these virtues they might be able to get a job, but they probably won't be able to hold one. And without a job it's very hard to thrive. That's their problem. But Barclay has a problem too. If he's a person of good character, he's got compassion and he's got justice and he's got patience that tempers his anger at sloppy work performance. But if he, or you, or Max DePree, or David Van Andel, or other community leaders have prudence, then all of them and all of us will wonder about one very straightforward question: What, exactly, do you do for people who seemingly cannot hold a job? What address to this problem combines compassion, justice, temperance, and prudence?

Good character is the sum of our virtues. It's a basket of virtues. Virtues are dispositions to tell the truth, feel compassion, keep promises, express thanks, and take responsibility. They are what make Jimmy Stewart admirable and Colin Powell electable. We all need them just to share a road safely.

But we need to face a tough question about all this. Are virtues inevitably religious? Can we be good without God? And if people disagree about the answer to this question—as they do— how can we move forward with public programs of character education and reform? Is it really possible for people of various religions and irreligions, various philosophies and worldviews, various visions of life and its meaning—is it really possible for such folk to come together on something as basic as character?

Doris Smedes and the guy in the gas station don't agree about basic virtues, do they?

The leaders of the Southern Baptist Church and the leaders of the death metal group Cannibal Corpse—they really see life somewhat differently, don't they?

How would anybody write a character document they'd all sign? And suppose nobody could write such a document. Does it follow that we ought to give up on the project of making moral judgments?

Cornelius Plantinga, Jr.

Chapter 4

Character Matters II:
No Safe Harbor

Toward the end of my lecture yesterday, I said that certain complications and questions arise within the moral life not in spite of having good character, but because of having it. The prudent person who really wants to employ the unemployable faces a struggle of soul and mind that a less conscientious person doesn't bother about. Moral dilemmas arise for people who care about morality. The rude guy at the gas station who pulls the nozzle out of your hand and tells you he really doesn't care what you think about it— that guy probably isn't going to toss and turn in his bed, agonizing over moral dilemmas. We may imagine that life for him is a little simpler.

Intertwining of good and evil

But, in fact, you never know. People are complex creatures. I think it's fair to say that almost nobody is as bad as we think. After all, it's terribly hard to be bad through and through. Being bad takes energy. Being *very* bad takes intelligence and persistence. Some badness takes courage. For instance, it takes courage to stick up a bank. Or, if you think that courage in the service of evil really isn't courage at all—if you think that the end contaminates the means— I think you will nonetheless concede that elsewhere in that bank robber's life you might find something good. Bad people often have shockingly good things going on in their lives. One of Lawrence Sanders' characters says, "I've had a lot of experience with hard cases, and I've learned one thing about them: None is completely bad. A rapist can be devoted to a sick mother. A safecracker can help support his church. (Money is one thing he has.) Even a murderer can drag a kid out of a burning house. None of us is one-dimensional." It's safe to say that nobody is as bad as we think. But it's also safe to say that nobody is as good as we think.

Hypocrisy is better than indifference, as we saw yesterday, but genuine goodness is better still. And yet it's sometimes hard to tell genuine goodness from hypocrisy. The reason is that a hypocrite is a kind of actor. (The Greek noun *hypocrites* means literally a play-actor.) A hypocrite is a kind of actor who works not on a stage or a screen where the medium itself lets us know that pretense is the order of the day; no, a hypocrite does his stuff right out in the middle of daily life. He's an actor working incognito, and he may be very good at what he does. A hypocrite may in fact be good enough to convince himself. Put it like this: An actor pretends, a hypocrite deceives, and one of the first persons a hypocrite deceives is himself. Only a beginning hypocrite or a recovering one understands that he's a fraud. Given his remarkable powers of self-deception, your truly committed hypocrite, your really deep-dish hypocrite, is a very sincere person.

The fact is that nobody is as good as you think. Everybody carries secrets. This is true even of people you'd never suspect. I once read of a priest who regularly heard the confessions of middle-aged nuns. These were people who literally led cloistered lives and who therefore had small occasion for the big, juicy, Miami vices that are the primary colors of contemporary TV. When he was asked what it was like to hear confession from such gentle folk, the priest replied that it was like being stoned to death with popcorn.

But who knows whether even nuns tell the whole truth?

The fact is that in human character, good and evil are twisted and twined around each other to such a degree that it is often remarkably hard to tell where the one leaves off and the other begins. Indeed, people sometimes put good into the service of evil and evil into the service of good. You recall that in the film *Schindler's List*, Oskar Schindler saves Jews not only because he has some justice and compassion in him but also because he is a highly accomplished liar and cheater. The world's literature is full of people who are remarkable along this line. To paraphrase Dickens, they are the best of people and the worst of people. They are simultaneously courageous, charitable, lustful, and deceitful.

All this is true, and the discovery of it is one of the fruits of maturity. It is also one of the fruits of education, and the knowledge that this is so ought to keep our character education from becoming hokey. (Maybe it ought to have kept the advertisers of Bill Bennett's *Book of Virtues* education course from advertising it as a form of entertainment.)

Character is serious business. Character is complex. It's full of shadows as well as light. This might mean that we are not content to teach compassion by having cheerleaders rise up at school assemblies during compassion week and yell "Gimme a C! Gimme an O!" We may need to take things a little further than that.

Starting with the ABCs

Good character education will eventually get to see some of the complexities. But let me now add that in character education, as in all education, complexity may not be the place to start. There is no point in dazzling youngsters with moral dilemmas when they haven't even learned the moral rules whose apparent conflict *creates* the dilemma. Gilbert Meilaender writes about this in his book *The Theory and Practice of Virtue*. He knows as well as we do that someday a properly instructed human being will wonder whether somebody ought to frame one man to save the lives of five. But few of us, thank God, have to face such agonizing dilemmas. Moreover they will be dilemmas for us only if we have had a basic education in moral thinking.

The idea is to start more simply. The idea is to start with the ABCs before you diagram complex sentences. Learn basic baseball, says Meilaender, before worrying about the dilemma presented by intentionally walking a good hitter.

So, too, in moral education. Maybe it would be wise to begin not with the agonies of triage, but with the beauty of some basic moral attitudes and tendencies: "to act honestly, speak truthfully, prize fairness, esteem courage, honor parents, care for the weak, plan for descendants, delight in mercy" (Meilaender).

People who have learned these things will be ready one day to worry about lifeboat dilemmas. But first they need Goodness 101. In fact, we need to know the good and to love it in order to develop any real conscience. Without conscience, thinking about morality is only an indoor sport. Borrowing a whole line of thinking from Plato, Meilaender concludes this: If you stimulate the intellect with dilemmas before you have thoroughly instructed the conscience, you don't really have a shot at helping a person become good. All you're doing is helping her to become shrewd. And the thought of spending one's life educating people to become shrewd is a pretty desolating thought.

What we want in moral education, then, is a movement from simplicity to complexity. The goal, I believe, is to come out on the other side. The goal is eventually to consider moral ambiguities, complexities, and dilemmas, and to consider them honestly. But we won't want to get stuck in them. Even after considering them, a person of good character will still want "to act honestly, speak truthfully, prize fairness, esteem courage, honor parents, care for the weak, plan for descendants, and delight in mercy." She will want to do these things with the "second simplicity" of a grownup— a deep simplicity, an educated simplicity, a simplicity that lies *beyond* complexity.

Suppose that, in the spirit of this second simplicity, we stipulate that good character makes life livable inside our own skin. Suppose we stipulate that good character is an advantage to our neighbors, and that they feel amiable when we've got it. Suppose we stipulate further that good character helps us find the good in others. The reason this works, as Caroline Simon has recently written in a wonderful book entitled *The Disciplined Heart,* is that a person of good character possesses respect for others. Respecting other persons means taking the time to see their goodness (*respectare* means "to look again," "to take a second look"). Finally, suppose we stipulate that good character both generates good society and benefits from it. Good character in individual persons helps to make society more civil, more humane, more harmonious—all of which tends, in a virtuous circle, to generate more good character.

Whose values? Whose virtues?

Given all these stipulations, let me add that if you believe in God, you will believe that good character fits people who have been made in God's image, and that good character is therefore as much of a gift as a calling. If you believe in Jesus Christ, you will believe further that good character fits people who have been resurrected with Christ in their baptism.

But here's the rub and the main topic for today. Not everybody believes in God. Most people in the country say they do, but not everybody. Even fewer are convinced that their lives belong to Jesus Christ. Is it really possible for believers in various religions and unbelievers in various religions, for people of various religions and irreligions, various philosophies and worldviews, various visions of life and its meaning—is it really possible for such folk to come together on something as basic and personal as character?

Back in 1992, at one of the seminal events of the character education movement, a group of ethicists and educators meeting in Aspen, Colorado, issued a statement called the "Aspen Declaration on Character Education." This statement specifies the "Six Pillars of Character" to be instilled in our youth, namely, trustworthiness, respect, responsibility, justice, caring, and civic responsibility. The declaration further says that these pillars—these core ethical values rooted in democratic society—transcend cultural, religious, and socioeconomic differences.

Is that really so?

We live in a pluralist society that has not just one culture, but many, and lots of them are not Christian, and lots are not formally religious. Indeed, one of the central paradoxes of the contemporary world is that we have seldom been more unified by means of transportation and communication and commercial images, and yet seldom more balkanized by philosophy and religion and self-understanding. We are one world and we are also a galaxy of cultural worlds. Watch the major parades in New York City. One week it's the Children's Parade for Peace; the next week we have the Lesbian and Gay Pride Day Parade; and then the Krishna Procession, and the Queens Purim Procession, and the Armenian Martyrs' Day

Parade. Fifty major parades a year in New York City alone. A different parade every week and the same politicians standing along the curb wearing determined smiles. Are all these kinds of people going to agree on what good human character ought to look like?

Two kinds of pluralism

Here it's important to make a distinction that Richard Mouw offers in his book *Uncommon Decency.* What we have to notice, says Mouw, is that pluralism is itself plural. On the one hand, we have what we could broadly call cultural pluralism. Here we're talking about human differences of race, gender, ethnicity, language, social status, and geographical origin. Cultural pluralism is mainly what gets paraded along Fifth Avenue in New York, and, although it may matter somewhat when character is being discussed, it doesn't often matter decisively. If you ask an African-American man from Detroit and an Irish-American woman from Boston and a Hispanic-American teenager from San Antonio whether kindness is morally better than cruelty, you will likely get just one answer.

The same goes for men and women. It's true that they look at life a little differently, according to some studies. The reason, for instance, that the children of Israel wandered in the wilderness for forty years is that the men weren't willing to ask for directions. Men and women do life a little differently, and so do peasants and university professors.

The same goes for other groups represented in cultural pluralism. But these differences don't usually bear on basic morality very directly—with a few notable exceptions, such as those cases in which moral convictions lie at or near the base of such cultural identity as that of gay and lesbian groups.

Generally speaking, it's when we turn to a second kind of pluralism that we cut a little closer to the bone. Here (to use Mouw's language) we have a pluralism of "Worldviews and Value Systems." We find around us an amazing array of philosophies and religions and ideologies. We find not only Protestants, Catholics, and Jews, but also Buddhists, Muslims, and Hindus. We find radical feminism, materialist and humanist secularism; we find followers of occult philosophies and of all those spiritualities à la carte that spring up in Marin County, California. Look around town and you can also find people whose worldview is essentially political—liberal, conservative, neo-conservative. And the list could be extended.

It's here in the pluralism of worldviews and value systems that we find not only real and interesting differences among people, but also really basic ones. And this isn't even counting the differences *inside* most of the groups I've mentioned. If a Gentile reads the books of Chaim Potok, for example, she will discover some tensions inside Judaism that threaten the peace even between people who love each other—such as parents and children.

And, of course, the same goes for differences inside Christianity: There doesn't appear to be just one Christian position on abortion, for example, or on homosexuality, or on character education in public schools. Christians differ on what to think about the world's other great religions. Some Christians believe that all the adherents of other religions plus all secularists will end up in hell—"where they belong," such folk might add; other Christians say maybe not; still others say definitely not. Some very liberal Christians believe that Christianity is no more true or false than any other religion or irreligion they might have settled upon.

So in a world, even within this country, of scores of religions and irreligions, of dozens of philosophies of life that go with these religions or else go on their own—given such worldview pluralism, how will we come together on a matter so sensitive, so basic, so personal, so seemingly religious as human character?

Five observations

I have five observations to make in addressing this question. I don't say I'm going to answer the question. That would be a pretty foolhardy thing to say. But I am going to address it.

First observation

The simple, empirical fact is that people of very different worldviews actually do agree on most core virtues. Read around in the literature, and you will discover that at the level of making virtue lists (we're not talking yet about how to apply them in concrete situations, though even there we'd find a significant overlap) people who are otherwise philosophically and religiously different from each other widely agree on basic virtues.

We can see this by reading about school districts that have adopted character education programs. What they typically do, so the literature tells me, is simply to take some steps to establish consensus. They publish a statement—maybe one something like that of the Michigan Board of Education—and then they say to their constituents that they propose to teach compassion, justice, self-control, and prudence in school. They ask for response. Is this OK with everybody? they ask. Does anybody object? Anybody want to add a few more virtues to the list? Anybody want to trade patience for forgiveness?

After a time of consensus building, the district adopts a program. If people object, the district officials respond by saying that they have a consensus and here's how it turned out. They add that they will follow the consensus and teach the virtues it has settled upon. They wish dissenters well, and then they start the new program of character education, secure in the knowledge that they have solid support from constituents.

Second observation

Lots of people who want public virtue, and who want it taught or at least assumed in the nation's schools, have very religious reasons for their view. And that's just fine. In fact, the nation's students need to understand the huge role that religious faith has traditionally had in motivating morality, including social morality, and the social morality that most of us in this country admire. Why are life, liberty, and the pursuit of happiness inalienable rights? Because we don't give them to each other. These rights are endowed upon us by our Creator, says the Declaration of Independence. Lots of people in this country think the Declaration got it right and, of course, a citizen is entitled to agree with the Declaration and to say so.

The founding fathers and mothers of our country believed

both in human depravity and in human virtue. On the one hand, they knew that human hearts are corrupt. They therefore instituted in the Constitution a set of checks and balances against pride and the lust for power. But they also knew that the awareness of our corruption was a good awareness. Only someone who knows what a straight stick looks like can tell when one is bent. (Or, as somebody at Calvin College once put it, "Any Calvinist who believes in human depravity can't be *all* bad.")

So the founders (I'm thinking now of some of the Federalist papers of James Madison in particular) thought what most of us think. They thought that we are people of both light and shadows and that we need to encourage the light because we can't have good society without it. For example, if we are corrupt, we will vote all the scoundrels into office and hound out the honest folks.

Indeed, it's not hard to find in the founders, and in the abolitionist movement, and in the great statements of great presidents such as Abraham Lincoln, standard religious assumptions about human covenant, about the image of God in human beings, and about how sinning against a neighbor is also sinning against God because our neighbor is God's child. It thus appears that one perfectly good way to be an American on the character issue is to see it religiously. Some of the most inspiring Americans in history have seen and spoken of character religiously.

Martin Luther King, Jr., for example, said he dreamt of a nation in which "all God's children—white children and black children—would be judged not by the color of their skin but by the content of their character." Almost everything this great American did in public was religiously based. At a speech at the Van Andel Museum in Grand Rapids back on April 24, Stephen Carter, the Yale law professor who writes on character issues, reminded us that King and his followers fought for civil rights religiously. Most of King's sermons were speeches and most of his speeches were sermons. As you recall, nobody objected that he was bringing religion into the public square. Nobody said to him that he had to quit talking about God in public. Nobody said that he was a minister and therefore disqualified to speak outside church.

When Martin Luther King, Jr., said to his followers, "Start marching. March on the ballot box till we seat a Congress that fears God," people got inspired. Something started to rise up inside them. This happened even to a lot of people who did not believe in God. They simply sheared off King's religious motive and manner of expression and embraced the sheer justice of his cause. As for believers, they knew that King's cause was a righteous cause because it was God's cause. And they knew something else too. They knew what every tyrant knows: Religiously based morality is powerful because the backing for it is transcendent and therefore relativizes human loyalties. In particular, it relativizes loyalty to unjust governments. "The Letter from the Birmingham Jail" is a masterpiece of ethical thinking for this very reason. What King says there is that a religious person will look at an unjust law and reject it in the interest of obeying a higher law. What King does with this statement is to challenge ministers to shun the idolatry of simple-minded obedience to bad law.

Martin Luther King, Jr., inspired the devotion of good people and the enmity of bad people not in spite of his references to God and Scripture but in large part because of them. And I guess that's OK to do in public in America. One way to tell is to notice that Martin Luther King, Jr., is a national hero on a level with Washington and Lincoln, with his own day set aside to honor his courage and achievement. One of his main achievements was to shame bigots into seeing their character flaws.

The upshot is that if somebody wants to back up their interest in character education or character development with appeal to their religious beliefs, that's just fine to do. It's just fine to do in public. That's free speech in a free country, and the person who does it will probably inspire some of his or her fellow citizens and make some others squirm. That's just the way life often goes— politically, religiously, and every other important way. The fact is that Martin Luther King, Jr., was never more characteristically American than when he backed up his appeal for justice by reference to God.

[*An insert,* prompted by reflection on a discussion that followed this lecture:

But don't religiously backed moralities have much to answer for in the way of cruelty, intolerance, murder, and general nastiness? They do. What follows is that a person who calls himself religious, as I do, must therefore do so with shame as well as with joy. But, then, that's also true of everybody who calls herself "American" or "political." Religion taken narrowly (to include phenomena coordinate with, say, Christianity and Islam) has done both great harm and great good, and inevitably so, given that religion is a powerful engine of human movements, and given that, like such other powerful engines as politics, it is subject to corruption. The same religion that builds hospitals also lights fires under heretics. Religion, defined in this narrower and conventional way, is thus like Congress. It's hard to answer the question whether congressional initiatives are good or bad. You first want to ask, Which ones?

Something similar is true if we adopt a broader definition of religion so that it includes (as was proposed in our discussion Tuesday noon) Nazism, Soviet and Chinese Communism, and other phenomena that are nonconventionally religious or even atheist. Then, too, religion has motivated great wickedness. But, once again, it's hard to make this out as a real objection to religion. For on this broad definition of religion (the one in which passionate atheists qualify) "being religious" looks a lot like "being human," or, perhaps, "being non-stoically human." After all, one characteristic way to be human is to adopt strong and life-organizing convictions and to join with others in expressing them, acting upon them, and lobbying for them. It is moreover characteristic of passionate human beings that they will seek to get some of their convictions codified (as in the case of either more restrictive or more permissive abortion laws, or as in the case of civil rights laws) so that others must acknowledge them too. Most passionate people are "religious" in this sense. Though it's hard to make this out as an objection to religion, it's of course crucial to reflect on the question whether our passions motivate us toward good or ill.]

Third observation

Suppose that a lot of Americans get their morality from religion (in the narrow sense of religion, which is how I'm using the term) and that both history and the First Amendment tell us it's just fine to live that way and to say publicly that you do.

My third observation is that it doesn't follow that public school teachers should do it, or should do it as freely as they would off the job. Their position is, after all, not that of prophet, but of instructor, and the contract for getting along together in a pluralist setting under the First Amendment adds a big wrinkle where the grounding of morality is concerned. The wrinkle is that although lots of people do get their morality from their religion, the hookup between them is sensitive in school because religious people don't want their child moralized according to the tenets of some religion other than theirs, and non-religious people don't want their child moralized according to the tenets of any religion at all.

In a new book entitled *Finding Common Ground: A First Amendment Guide to Religion in Public Schools*, Charles Haynes addresses this tender matter with considerable wisdom. Here's what he says:

> The civic and moral values widely held in our society, such as honesty, caring, fairness, and integrity, *can* be taught without invoking religious authority. In public schools, where teachers may neither promote nor denigrate religion, these values *must* be taught without religious indoctrination.

Then he adds this:

> At the same time, teaching core values may not be done in such a way as to suggest that religious authority is unnecessary or unimportant.

There's the pair of statements, and the conjunction of them gives us a very subtle position. Do not indoctrinate, says Haynes. Do not invoke religious authority for your core virtues. At the same time, never say that where these core virtues are concerned, religious authority is unnecessary or unimportant.

I read Haynes as offering counsel on how to respond to a central question: Do you need God in order to be good? Haynes' counsel is that if that question arises in a public school setting and you are in charge, do not say yes. That would be theistic indoctrination. After all, lots of nonreligious people appear to be good people who love justice, compassion, and prudence just as much as anybody else.

On the other hand, says Haynes (if I understand him right), when the question, Do you need God to be good? arises, don't say no either. Why not? Because for all we know and for all we may say in a First Amendment setting, the fact that people are good without believing in God might be irrelevant as to whether they actually *need* God in order to be good. Maybe—again, for all we know or may say in a First Amendment setting in school—maybe people have been created by God with an ineradicable conscience, but they don't always know it, or don't want to know it, or don't like the thought of it very well. But if God does exist—which is a live possibility—then all this is a very possible scenario.

So here's the dilemma. If you say yes, you need God to be good, you offend disbelievers in God who ground their morality some other way and who may think that the whole idea of God is irrelevant, crazy, or dangerous. On the other hand, if you say no, you don't need God to be good, you offend believers who think that God is himself the supreme good in the universe and that God ultimately creates and sustains every human impulse toward virtue, including all those generated by God-given conscience in people who don't even believe in God.

So where does that leave us? If to a question like, Do you need God to be good? you can't really teach a yea or a nay answer, doesn't this imply that the only alternative is a kind of agnosticism about morality? Or a kind of relativism? If we can't agree on the source of morality, on the ground of morality, shouldn't we just shut up about it?

That's what some folks think. Back on February 11, 1997, the *NBC Evening News* did a segment on character education in the schools saying that character movements were spreading across the country and that one in five public schools now has a character program of some kind. Various people said how fine the movements were, how they had changed the atmosphere in school, etc. But one observer, a Cornell University professor, took another position. This whole movement is silly, he said. The reason is that if you model kindness, and read stories about kindness, and praise kindness and reprove unkindness, you will soon have your little kingdom of kindness toppled by one simple question—the question, why?

Some student or some high school English teacher whose head is full of Nietzsche is going to ask, Why be kind? And then you'll be stuck, said the professor from Ithaca, because we have no answer to that question.

Fourth observation

My fourth observation is that this professor is very wrong. There are some perfectly straightforward answers to the question and not nearly all of them require an appeal to religious authority. One or two of these answers are, I admit, embarrassingly simple, but that's nothing against them.

The main (nonreligious) answer to the question, Why be kind? is that it is right to be kind. It is good to be kind. Indeed, it is excellent to be kind. Of course this is a general assertion, and of course there may be unusual circumstances where our kindness will be misinterpreted, or exploited, or fouled up in some other way so that we temporarily have to suspend it. Even so, we would not then think that the only alternative was cruelty. To have to suspend kindness doesn't mean that we have to suspend everything.

General moral truths are generally true—no more and no less. But that doesn't make them false. That doesn't even make them doubtful. And it surely doesn't make kindness as a character trait anything less than it is—morally lovely.

Let me explore this a little further. Moral truths are defensible and teachable in more than one way. The main answer to the question, Why be kind? is simply that it is very good to be that way.

But this isn't the only relevant answer. In a pragmatic society we might take a pragmatic approach. To a skeptic who says, Why should I be kind? we might say, for example, that if you are unkind to others, they will be unkind back to you, and that this will be unpleasant for you. What goes around comes around. You generally reap what you sow. It's in your own interest to be kind to others.

But suppose we are dealing with a person who is a true and unenlightened egotist. Suppose our skeptic says, "I'd like others to be kind to me, all right. I can see the benefit there. But at the same time I'd like to be free to be secretly unkind to them—betraying them, for example, in case it will make me come out ahead. Why shouldn't I try to arrange things so that others trust me and are kind to me while I secretly undermine them for my own advantage?"

Why not? I can think of no answer more to the point than Doris Smedes' remark to the man at the gas pump. We shouldn't betray people who are kind to us because such behavior is contemptible. And if the skeptic then says, "But, lady, I really don't give a damn what you think," then we have indeed reached an impasse. If somebody really thinks that indifference is better than kindness, or that cruelty is better than kindness, or that dishonesty is better than honesty, we don't have anywhere to go with such a person. Morally speaking, we can't persuade such a person of anything. If a person can't see that 2+1 is 3, how will we get on with the rest of arithmetic? If water sticks in his throat, what will we use to wash it down?

The reason we do have consensus on basic virtues despite moral skeptics (some of whose skepticism is academic and subject to revision when they themselves have been betrayed) is that the goodness of a virtue like kindness is self-evident. A person who cannot see this is like a person who is color-blind or tone-deaf. Of course people disagree (and disagree heartily) whether some particular action (keeping a person on a job that he cannot do, for example) counts as an instance of kindness, but the people who disagree do so *while agreeing* that there really is such a thing as kindness and that it really is a very good thing.

Courts sometimes (quite rarely, say the experts I've been reading) have to judge that a person who did something cruel didn't at that time know the difference between right and wrong and is therefore not guilty by reason of insanity. A judgment of this kind is instructive because it reminds us of the common wisdom that passes into common law, namely, that a person who doesn't know that cruelty is wrong has lost touch with reality. A person who really can't see that it is wrong to torture a child for the fun of it isn't merely in error. This is a person who is insane.

I believe it's important to notice that even if the skeptic or the child abuser before the court is sincere in his conviction, we may still have to judge him wrong. Sincerity doesn't get to veto justice or kindness. Recall that classic hypocrisy is sincere. So is insanity—indeed, this is one of its more terrifying features. The guy in the gas station may have been sincere too. He may *really* not have cared about fairness. But this doesn't mean in the least that his unfairness isn't contemptible. It's contemptible no matter what he thinks. If this seems unduly straightforward or dogmatic, think again of the civil rights movement. Bigots sincerely opposed and hated what Martin Luther King, Jr., was striving for. The right way to assess that state of affairs is not to say that King was for desegregation, but his opponents were sincerely opposed to it, with the result that we just can't tell who was right. Not at all. King was right in his mission, and those who tried to thwart him were wrong, and sane people of good will came to see it and to pass laws that stated what they saw.

Let me cite Stephen Carter again. Law is all congealed morality. Every law says either, You must do this even if you don't want to, or else it says, You must not do this even if you want to. Our wants are important but not final where morality is concerned because, like other important things, our wants can get corrupted.

Law is congealed morality. And we can get some idea of where the commonly discerned lines of morality fall by following the trajectory of the law. Don't steal. Do give to charities. Don't lie.

Do keep your promises. Don't assault or kill. Do show compassion to a wounded stranger. In most jurisdictions, the law doesn't *oblige* you to help the wounded stranger, but "Good Samaritan Laws" often give us a lead nonetheless by specifying certain special immunities for people who, let's say, try to help but end up harming the stranger instead. By such provisions the law says in effect, Do try to help.

The country's founding documents—and especially the documents around them—give us guidance toward the common good in a pluralistic society. The same is true of common and statute law. But the biggest lead of all is given by the active moral consensus of ordinary people who have a conscience that tells them something about kindness, cruelty, justice, and love.

Fifth observation

But is this really so? Do people actually make the kinds of moral judgments and admire the sort of character that I've been speaking of? Aren't there actually quite a few folks who simply dispute the existence of the sort of objective good and evil that I've been assuming? My fifth observation is that there are indeed some moral skeptics out there, but that their position is troubled by internal difficulties and that, in any case, we who have to take public positions on moral issues will find no safe harbor in skepticism.

Let's go back to our moral skeptic, to the person who thinks it's impossible to define objective good and evil. This is a person who rejects the idea that some acts are good and some are evil regardless of what we think about the matter. Predictably enough, skeptics think that the whole enterprise of character education is bogus. They think it's bogus because in order to form character you have to agree upon the virtues that you'd like to see in a person's character, and this agreement isn't possible. Why isn't it possible? Well, say the skeptics, each person properly chooses for herself what counts as a virtue, and the same goes for each culture, with the result that you can't really have any moral teaching from one individual to another, and you can't really have any cross-cultural teaching. Individuals are morally autonomous and so are cultures.

According to this skeptical view, the attempt to inculcate virtue is therefore a kind of imperialism. You are morally trespassing the sacred boundaries of another person's autonomy or another culture's autonomy if you attempt character education, and you ought to quit this trespassing and mind your own business.

There are names for these theories, as you know from looking at Mary Midgley's lucid little book *Can't We Make Moral Judgments?* The view that each person is morally autonomous Midgley calls "subjectivism" (referring to a single human "subject"). More fully put, subjectivism is the view that moral judgments are validated by and limited to any particular person who generates them or adopts them. Each person decides for himself what's right or wrong. Each person is her own moral lawgiver. So if John thinks that cheating on a math test is simply part of the thrill of victory in academe while Joe thinks that cheating on a math test breaks trust with his instructor and other classmates, they could both be right. For according to subjectivism, cheating at math is "right for John" and it is "wrong for Joe."

The other theory is what Midgley calls "moral relativism." Moral relativism is about cultures, not individuals, and it holds that moral judgments, like cultural fashions and manners, are validated by and limited to any particular culture that generates or adopts them. Culture A, for example, favors routine clitoridectomy for twelve-year-old girls while culture B finds the practice sexist, abusive, and unjust. According to moral relativism, both are right, and the reason is that each culture is morally autonomous. Thus clitoridectomy is "right for culture A" and it is "wrong for culture B."

I suppose that most people instinctively suspect that there may be enough screws loose in these ideas that they would be hard to fasten down. But lest anyone think that subjectivism and relativism are only textbook theories that no live persons actually hold, we might consider the June 27 issue of *The Chronicle of Higher Education,* which Dean Miller recently called to my attention. One article tells of the experience of Kay Haugaard, a professor at Pasadena

City College, who has been teaching Shirley Jackson's short story "The Lottery" for a number of years. This is a story, as you may recall, that is set in what appears to be an ordinary American country village where people are "warm" and "loving" and "earnest." In this village there is an annual lottery that people conduct with all the seriousness of a ritual. Some of the surrounding villages have stopped their lotteries, but not this one. In this particular village the Hutchinson family—father, mother, son Dave, and twelve-year-old daughter Tess—arrive for the annual drawing. And when the father draws a ticket for the whole family, "nothing prepares the first-time reader for what happens next: Everyone, including four-year-old Dave, attacks Tess Hutchinson and stones her to death." The lottery turns out to be a ritual of human sacrifice.

Professor Haugaard then remarks on student responses to the story. For years, she says, students always responded with shock. They were stunned, distressed, amazed. How could people who seemed so normal do something so horrific? they wanted to know. And then students and professor would speak together of the dangers of just "going along" with the crowd, of just buying into whatever practices people in your precinct think of as normal. In other words, they would rehearse the Huckleberry Finn moment of discovery that one's own culture is corrupt.

But Professor Haugaard reports that student attitudes have shifted. One student expressed mild surprise that this practice appeared to be occurring in the United States. Another said that the story was pretty boring till the end. She said the sacrifice part was "neat." Another student said that he thought the story was all right, but that he wasn't too excited about it. An elementary school teacher who was taking the class allowed that the ending was pretty surprising, but that, hey, the folks in this town had their reason for the sacrifice—namely, to make their crops grow. Not one student in this most recent discussion of the story could get herself to condemn the villagers' action. They all took it for granted that some people do things one way, and some another, and who are we to judge? A 50-year-old nurse in the class reported that she taught a course in multicultural understanding and that in this course she instructs students not to judge any parts of other people's culture.

There it is. That's moral relativism. And Professor Haugaard's report is followed in the same issue of *The Chronicle* by a piece from a Hamilton College professor, Robert L. Simon, who tells of students who claim personally to dislike what the Nazis were up to but then append a tolerant question: "But who's to say they were morally wrong?" Professor Simon remarks that students in his classes in recent years have asked similar questions about apartheid, slavery, and ethnic cleansing. These students take it for granted, they take it as self-evident, that we may never even criticize, let alone condemn, the moral views or practices of some other culture—not the culture of Mississippi slavery in the 1850s, not pre-Mandelan apartheid in South Africa, not the Nazi idea of a final solution to the problem of racial heterogeneity. Students will not condemn these practices as morally wrong because to them such condemnation amounts to moral imperialism.

My own view is that if a moral theory causes you to suspend judgment on what the Nazis did, this outcome serves as a *reductio ad absurdum* on the theory. A theory can't be right if it leads to this outcome.

But for anybody who needs to go a bit further, consider Mary Midgley's analysis. The title of the book *Can't We Make Moral Judgments?* comes from a day in philosophy class when Midgley had been lecturing on a moral topic and perhaps expressing indignation about a particular injustice. At some point a student raised her hand and said, "But Professor Midgley, surely it's always wrong to make moral judgments!" And Midgley goes on to muse over that student's moral judgment, which so neatly negates itself in the very act of making it.

As she proceeds, without invoking any religious dogma or creed, Professor Midgley provides us with excellent reasons for rejecting subjectivism and relativism. I will summarize her analysis, but I urge you to read it for yourselves if you haven't already done so.

The first thing to notice, says Midgley, is that subjectivism and relativism look like they come from the same factory, and so people jumble them together. But in fact they are brutally incompatible with each other, and each by itself breeds remarkable paradoxes. Some of the difficulties in the neighborhood can be brought home by reflecting on the paralyzed position of a subjectivist (Sartre, say, or Ayn Rand) who thinks that nobody should take a moral position because of outside influence from others and who wishes to influence others to think so too.

Or, consider the status of a moral revolutionary in some culture—a culture, for example, in which everybody but the revolutionary favors routine clitoridectomy for twelve-year-olds. What is the contemporary outsider to make of this clash? Whose position should he endorse? The revolutionary's subjective judgment is clearly incompatible with her culture's judgment and yet, according to the jumbled position that conjoins relativism and subjectivism, both judgments must be right. The revolutionary who thinks clitoridectomy abominable is right and so is her culture, which thinks it's just fine.

Moral clashes

In general, moral clashes give the relativist a headache. He can hardly endorse intracultural moral reform since, according to his baseline, the status quo position is valid in that culture. So what would the relativist think of Martin Luther King's march on the ballot box? The status quo position was segregation, and since it was the predominant view of the culture, the relativist has to think it was right. But King and his followers rejected that view. Now it appears that the relativist is stuck: In order to endorse reform he needs to endorse Dr. King's position. But in order to be a relativist he also needs to endorse segregation, which was the dominant cultural position. So where must the relativist stand when looking at a reform movement inside a culture?

And what about cross-cultural clashes? Suppose culture A attacks culture B in order to reform it. Culture A is reformist by nature. Culture B is resistant to reform. Whose side shall the relativist take?

Moreover, what entitles the outsider to any judgment whatsoever on all these matters? He can't even say, "That's *right* for them" or "That's *right* for her" without violating his own exclusionary rule against making moral judgments about other cultures and persons. His safest and most consistent course is apparently to keep still about moral matters altogether.

Which he almost surely will not do and which is why books like Midgley's are so helpful.

Tolerant people of good will are much tempted by moral subjectivism and relativism. These positions look like respectful positions. "Live and let live," they seem to say. Unhappily, they are riddled with paradoxes, and they appear to lead toward the bland tolerance of such horrors as human sacrifice and Nazi genocide.

Moreover, there's a point here that is particularly important to see if you are a person who must take a public position on touchy moral issues. The point is that subjectivism and relativism offer us no refuge from moral criticism. Once more, they look as if they might offer this advantage, and they therefore look tempting to beleaguered public officials. In such a case we may be tempted to say, "Look, here we are amidst a number of clashing individuals in the public square and a number of clashing cultures. Let's keep the peace by maintaining moral neutrality. We'll fold our arms and say that everybody is right and that we refuse to judge amongst them. People will praise our tolerance, nobody will accuse us of being judgmental, and we will enjoy the gentle murmur of public approval wherever we go."

Not so. Some people will be horrified by our ethical neutrality. They will regard it not merely as paradoxical and confused; they will regard it as spineless. To them, to lots of people (perhaps including Professors Haugaard and Simon), the refusal to condemn slavery, or apartheid, or human sacrifice, or clitoridectomy—or a dozen other things—is weak and cowardly. If we refuse to take moral stands, we trap ourselves in the terrible silence of the moderate masses that Martin Luther King feared so much. "We will have to repent in this generation," he wrote, "not merely for the hateful words and actions of the bad people, but also for the appalling silence of the good people."

Taking a moral position

My point is that there is no safe harbor. Refusing to judge is as much a moral stance as judging, and every bit as controversial. Trying to move safely outside the field of moral judgment, and therefore of character judgment, is like trying to move outside the universe. We do think morally, we must think morally, inevitably we will think morally. And the reason is that it's part of our very humanity to do so. We are creatures who know so very well what the word *ought* means that, unless we have been morally numbed, we will sometimes applaud human acts as noble, honorable, courageous, or compassionate, and we will applaud the human character that generates such acts. On the other hand, we will sometimes condemn acts as base, ignoble, unjust, or cruel, and we will also depreciate the kind of character that begets—or even tolerates—such acts. Taking a moral position in the public square is not only permissible but inevitable, and the reason is that it is inevitably human.

Of course there are ways of taking moral positions with tolerance, with civility, with respect for those with whom we disagree. There are ways of taking moral positions with good humor and self-irony and the sort of humility that is prepared to learn from those who have more light to shed. Indeed, it's part of good character to take moral positions in these ways.

But there's no way to *avoid* taking a moral position. There's no refuge where nobody will question or trouble us. We are all embarked on a moral adventure in which character matters, and the trick will be to sail together in some kind of decent formation even if, in a pluralistic setting, we don't agree in the least about our final destination.

Dr. James Davison Hunter
William R. Kenan Jr. Professor
of Sociology and Religious Studies
Director of The Post-Modernity Project
University of Virginia
Charlottesville, Virginia

Dr. James Davison Hunter is the William R. Kenan Jr. Professor of Sociology and Religious Studies at the University of Virginia. He also serves as the Director and Principal Investigator for The Post-Modernity Project, a research and teaching initiative concerned with contemporary social and cultural change.

Dr. Hunter has written seven books and a wide range of essays, articles, and reviews, all variously concerned with the problem of meaning and moral discourse in a time of political and cultural change in American life.

James Davison Hunter

Chapter 5

Education and the Challenge
of Cultural Conflicts
in a Democratic Society

Conflict in Gaston County

I want to begin with a quick story. A man by the name of Edwin West was the superintendent of schools in Gaston County, North Carolina. Mr. West and others had succeeded in winning a very competitive multi-million- dollar grant to bring the Gaston County schools into the twenty-first century. Gaston County is located in the Piedmont Region of western North Carolina. Historically a mining community, it is rural and, in general, poor. The purpose of the grant was to modernize the Gaston County school system in terms of its facilities, curricula, and resources. It was an exciting time.

What ended up happening was not so exciting. In fact, in the end it was tragic.

Some of the curricular innovations the school system was considering included such controversial programs as "outcome-based education." It was not long before certain citizens voiced their concern about the new curricula. A local pastor became involved and became something of a spokesperson for one side of this developing controversy, and within a very short time what began as a dispute among neighbors escalated. Two organizations that are culturally conservative, Citizens for Excellence in Education and the Christian Coalition, soon became involved. When that happened, two culturally liberal organizations, People for the American Way and the American Civil Liberties Union, also became involved, thus further escalating the controversy.

Almost from the beginning, the warring sides resorted to litigation. It was not long before the special-interest organizations which had become involved began to use what was happening in Gaston County as a mechanism for their own national fund-raising. The dispute became something of a crucible for many of the issues that these organizations are concerned about and for which they are fighting.

Within this context, election to the Board of Education in Gaston County was highly contested. Every penny that was spent by the board was analyzed scrupulously by all parties involved. Everyone involved sought to expose any hint of corruption. The animosity became so entrenched that some people even resorted to such tactics as anonymous threats. This dispute wound up playing itself out over a period of two and a half years. The end of the story is that the grant was eventually withdrawn.

I would like you to keep this story in mind as we move forward, in part because it is a very practical illustration of something that I want to talk about in a very abstract way. It will help you see some of the practical ways in which the abstract issues which I will be discussing get played out. Undoubtedly, this case provides a parallel illustration for many of you. There are many here who have experienced similar kinds of tensions, though perhaps not precisely in this way.

The big picture

As educators, we face the day-to-day dilemmas of running schools, managing faculty, and satisfying the educational needs of our community. By necessity, most of our daily work is highly pragmatic. Conferences like this allow us to step back from the business of the practical and reflect, consult with colleagues and peers, and, sometimes, regain perspective so that we can go back to the day-to-day, week-to-week responsibilities with a slightly different perspective or with some renewed enthusiasm or vision.

I would like to offer you a glimpse into the broader social and historical context within which you do your work. I would like to invite you to take a step back, perhaps further than you already have, to see a larger picture of the situation in which all of us find ourselves at the end of the twentieth century and at the dawn of the twenty-first century. Again, at one level, my remarks may appear irrelevant, given the day-to-day concerns that you have. But I am of the mind that we all need to have a firm grasp of our circumstances in order to act wisely and engage our responsibilities effectively. It is essential that we see clearly. My hope is to contribute to a broad and clear understanding of the larger framework of our present situation.

To this end, I want to address some of the key questions of our time: How does our society, in all its complexity, hang together? Against all the pressures that we face, how does our society keep from falling apart? More aptly, in such a society and in its present condition, what is the place and role of the school?

In our political tradition we speak of a unity that exists within our diversity: *E Pluribus Unum.* Yet today this notion is challenged; as our diversity continues to expand and our unity grows continuously weaker, we are forced to wonder if *E Pluribus Unum* can be maintained. Furthermore, as educators we seek to know how the school can acknowledge and reflect the *pluribus,* the diversity, yet also somehow sustain some kind of *unum,* a unity. Seeking such a balance has been part of the historic role and institutional mission of public education and, in many respects, it continues to be. In this way, my agenda deals with some very broad questions. I will be painting not just with a broad brush but with a roller. There will be lots of gaps to fill in.

I will examine some of the challenges, the principle pressure points facing schools as institutions of social and political vitality. That is, schools are often presented to us in formal political rhetoric as being central to the kind of society that we have and to sustaining the kind of society that we all want.

Culture wars

Let me start with where I think we are as a society at the end of the twentieth century. As a social scientist, I know that social change rarely, if ever, happens gradually, slowly, and perceptively.

Most social change that happens within a society, within a civilization, happens in lurches, fits, and starts.

I also know that change almost never takes place without a conflict. It is one of the givens. So here we have a conflict, what I have called a "culture war." What does it mean? Of what is it a symbol? What does it mark? The answer to these questions has everything to do with the very nature of conflict itself. If conflict is a sign, if it is pointing to something else, what is it? The way in which most of us encounter the culture wars is through public policy disputes—angry rhetorical exchanges about abortion, homosexuality, gay rights, funding for the arts, church-state issues, disputes over the nature of the family, sexuality values in the schools, condom distribution, and so on. The culture warring is being waged in most of the domestic policy issues of our day.

Upon close inspection, we realize that in fact these public policy disputes are really cloaking deeper debates about the nature and purpose of our major institutions. Take abortion, for example. Clearly implicit in this most divisive of issues is a debate over the nature of the family and the meaning of motherhood. The same is true with the arts. For instance, contemporary contention over government funding of what certain groups consider "obscene" art is more truly about the very symbols of national life. The same is true with education and faith. Public-policy debates tend to hide deeper institutional debates about the nature and purpose of our fundamental institutions, involving competing moral visions about how to order our public life.

Finally, when you look underneath the public-policy disputes, the institutional debates, and underneath the competing moral visions, what you find are radically different worldviews; that is, there exist different ideas of what is true, what is right, and what is good as well as how we come to know the true, right, and good. The crux of the matter is this: when a conflict reaches to such a deep level in society, it means that the very constituting terms of our civilization are undergoing a transformation. Our culture war signals an epoch-defining moment. To what? We do not know for sure, but there are some clues. The point I want to be clear is that our society is at a juncture of unprecedented social and historical change, the likes of which we have never before seen.

The character of our present moment becomes clearer by glimpsing into the American past. Clearly, at the time of the nation's founding there was cultural conflict as well. Anyone here who has a historical background knows this to be true. There was tension between the modern deists, the moderate enlightenment thinkers, and the radical enlightenment thinkers as well as between the Thomas Paynes, on the one hand, and the Jeffersons and the Madisons, on the other. There was an even deeper cultural rift at that time between the reformed Protestants and the moderate and radical enlightenment sympathizers. Public discourse reflecting those tensions was as vociferous as any heard today. The kind of *ad hominem* arguments that were made were harsh—cultural conflict went deep. There was a sense that the future of the nation was at stake.

In sum, cultural conflict is not new; we have seen it before. However, there are some crucial differences between the older versions of conflict and the kind we are currently experiencing.

For all the differences of belief and opinion that existed at the time of the founding, there was, nevertheless, common agreement regarding what generally constituted the public good. The public agreement upon which the new republic was founded two centuries ago drew from three sources: It drew from a tradition of civic republicanism, from a common Protestantism, and thirdly, it drew from an emerging tradition of Lockean liberalism, emphasizing individual freedom and individual rights. Civic republicanism was an attempt to revive many of the great classical Greek traditions based on reason and rationality and summed up in the notion of *res publica.* Protestantism was a very strong, vital, biblical culture whose understandings of truth and justice and the common good were rooted in revelation. And thirdly, there was the tradition of liberalism with a new emphasis upon the rights and liberties of the individual. These were the primary materials by which America constructed a common national story. The story was not perfect by any stretch of the imagination, but it was fairly coherent. It provided a vision of common life and, as such, it shaped the purpose of our major institutions. It also helped to integrate diverse actions in a fairly complex society. That story did not take away pain and suffering. That story did not take away stupidity, unfairness, or unkindness, but it did provide a moral context in which life (that is, collective life) could be lived in a meaningful way.

I would like to point out some of the other points of agreement during the time of the founding. First, agreement was in many ways predicated upon a white, Anglo-Saxon, Protestant establishment. Even where the establishment was not Protestant in conviction, it was Protestant in its cultural sensibilities, as the defining cultural influence emanated overwhelmingly from Northern Europe. Secondly, there was agreement about the nature of our basic institutions. There were no disputes about what constituted the family; there were some about science, but it was a fairly small institution at the time. Basic notions of decency and public order were largely agreed upon; on issues of sexuality, there was no dispute. Basic institutions existed without very much argument, if any at all. Thirdly, and I think almost as important as anything else, whether you were a moderate or a radical deist or whether you were a deeply committed reformed Protestant, there was also an agreement about the destiny of the nation. There was a sense that what was taking place in America at the end of the eighteenth century was of tremendous importance. The hand of Providence was resting upon the nation, and the future was bright.

A final factor that was unique about that time was that society existed on what we would call a human scale. That is, most of society at the time existed within a kind of rural, agricultural, and mercantile social structure. In these and many other ways, our society was very different then from what it is today.

In contrast, contemporary American society is much bigger than the founders ever imagined it would or could be. The white, Anglo-Saxon, Protestant establishment, if it has not been completely demolished, is on its way. The combination of cultural resources that the founders drew upon, civic republicanism, common Protestantism, and Lockean liberalism, was unique and historically contingent. That common culture has unraveled or is in the process of

unraveling. Today, those traditions are largely useless in construct-
ing any notions of the social order. The story that people lived by
then no longer rings true to an increasing number of people. In its
place are an increasing number of competing stories. As a result,
the sense of agreement about basic institutions has largely disinte-
grated. And perhaps more devastating than anything else, the sense
of destiny that once so profoundly shaped the nation and carried it
through periods of national crisis, the sense that America was a
shining example of freedom and progress to the rest of the world,
has largely disappeared.

What are the consequences of the disintegration of these various social and cultural agreements? Let me address how these major transformations play out in national life. First, there is a crisis of
identity that exists within every major institution of our society, a
crisis of identity that extends to the ideals by which those institutions define themselves and are shaped. Take higher education,
where notions of academic freedom and civility have increasingly
become platitudinous. They make great copy for alumni and fund-
raising ventures; but truth be known, higher education is increasingly fragmented and discordant. Very often, academics of opposing views will not talk to each other, and, when they do, it is often
in the most uncivil manner. Indeed, the most uncivil discourse
that I have heard in America happens in the academy.

Why is this? It is because the core of our understanding of
what is knowledge, of what is truth, of what is the purpose of
higher education, is being contested. As a result, the pursuit of
certain lines of inquiry may be viewed as sexist, racist, and oppres-
sive. There are certain things one can and cannot say within the
academy. In this way, the ideals of academic freedom and of knowledge itself are contested. And while they have always been contested, they are now contested at a level that we have not seen
before.

Secondly, there is cultural conflict in the wake of disintegrat-
ing public agreement. Previously, conflict centered on attempts to
create consensus; today, much of the conflict is a result of various
factions attempting to reimpose consensus. The center no longer

holds; the conflict is about reimposing a center—not re-creating one, but reimposing one.

Thirdly, the disintegration of consensus has generated enormous fear for the average person. Such anxiety exists among liberals as well as conservatives, blacks as well as whites.

A deep pessimism

The central finding of a recent national survey of American political culture was the existence of a deep pessimism about the future of America. Accompanying this pessimism was a deep disaffection with the major institutions of our society, especially government, the schools, and the family. In addition, and perhaps more sharply than anything else, we found an incredible disaffection and cynicism toward national leadership. At an emotional level, the pessimism and disaffection translated into fear.

Yet, probing deeper using multivaried analysis, researchers found that at heart is not necessarily a rejection of America. Most Americans still love America—they love its ideals and that for which it stands. They believe, though, that it is on the wrong track, that it is headed in the wrong direction, guided by leaders who are too often self-interested and utterly unconcerned with the common person. Again, the base line emotion is one of fear. There is a sense of decline in America, a sense of the institutions failing and a fear about the direction. The survey found that there are three institutions, three areas, that were especially of concern to Americans: morals and values, the family, and schools. Concern was equal in regard to each area.

Let us focus on the situation of education, for few other institutions find themselves right in the middle of the cultural discord as do schools. Schools tend to be a lightning rod, not only because they pass on knowledge and skills to young people in preparation for adulthood but also because of their symbolic power. Schools, as the institutional vehicle for public education, are volatile because of what they represent: Education is the central institution of modern society through which the social order is reproduced. Everything about the school, the curricula, the textbooks, the extracurricular

activities, and the like, all convey powerful symbols about the meaning of American life—what the nation has been, what it is, and
where it is going. Moreover, education represents the power of the
state itself in support of the symbols of our public culture. Because
public schools, in particular, are government schools, they represent the sanctions of the state, the blessing of the state itself. That
is why the conflict over schools was so great in Germany in the
1870s at the time of unification. What was called *Kulturkampf* centered on the schools. All of the questions about national identity
were focused on that institution. The schools were right at the
vortex of all of the conflicting pressures.

The same may be said of the situation of the schools in contemporary America. The crisis of identity in the schools is played
out in everyday life in many contexts and under the guise of many
different issues, with the pressures of fragmentation being extraordinary. And the central question remains the same: What is the
mission of the schools? What Edwin West found in Gaston County,
North Carolina, was that in a very short period of time, the fourteen people who were finally members of the Board of Education
represented fourteen different visions of what the schools should
be. He found himself no longer an educator, but a politician.

Clearly conflict emerges precisely over these issues of identity.
Again, using the example of outcome-based education, questions
of values clarification or moral education are seen more broadly.
What kind of magazines should there be in the school library, for
instance? What ought the schools teach about family life, sexuality, and religion? Our society has entered a time of unprecedented
transformation, and this transformation has created tremendous
pressures, not least upon the institution of elementary and secondary education. As educators, we confront these pressures primarily
through specific policy issues. As difficult as these issues are to
resolve on their own, when seen in the larger context, we realize
that they, in fact, may be impossible to resolve.

Western civilization

Let me return briefly to the larger transformation about which

I have been speaking. To see clearly what I have been arguing, one might ask the basic question in any high school: What is Western civilization? Western civilization—the quick and messy answer—is a kind of moral vision, a way of life that was animated primarily by moral visions that came out of Athens and Jerusalem. Whatever Western civilization has been, it is minimally a range of societies that have drawn their cultural resources—their justifications for art, law, medicine, public health, community life, and social order—from this odd, uneven, and oftentimes tense symbioses between Athens and Jerusalem. If Western civilization can be understood as being constituted by those animating visions, then Western civilization, at least as we have known it for the last couple of millennia, is coming to an end. Its foundations are rapidly becoming deconstructed: the foundations of reason and rational deliberation, classical Greek (and later Enlightenment) notions which indicate that there is in fact a natural order, and that if we just apply ourselves and our minds to that order, we can understand and discern it. As the foundations of reason are being deconstructed, so too are the foundations that have come out of Jerusalem. This is what the culture war is marking. The culture war is a closing parenthesis of an epic we have called Western civilization. Now we may celebrate this event or we may bemoan it, but let us be clear about one thing: there is not a lot we can do about it either way. There are sociological and historical dynamics at play over which we have little or no control. As the schools in which we work have become a crucible for many of the tensions and controversies of the culture war, there is little to do but ride out the historical moment.

The question we need to pose, and a question that I think has an answer with very practical implications, is what is at stake in the transformation? Obviously there is quite a bit at stake, but there are two main things I would like to mention—two things that have practical implications for everyone. At the broadest level, what is at stake are the basic ordering institutions of public life which, taken together, constitute what we call democracy. It is a given that all societies require some basic agreements or they fall apart. It is no less true for a democracy. There needs to be some basic, shared agreements—both procedural and substantive—for democracies to function. The agreements must be about how we achieve consent but also about what we are ultimately aiming for—agreements about what justice really means, what freedom really means. Once again, all of these things are contested today, the main consequence of which is an attempt to reimpose agreement through litigation.

That is what is so interesting about the Gaston County case. Within a very short time, the special-interest groups came in and provided a ready-made language of political dispute. The residents of Gaston County, worried for the welfare of their children and trying to understand a confusing situation, were drawn into the divisive polemics of politics by the scripted language of the special-interest groups. Immediately, this conflict was litigated, making persuasion virtually impossible. Litigation is ultimately about power politics, not persuasion. Litigation in a sense was a measure of their impatience, and our society's impatience, with the ambiguity that exists in our historical moment. (A historical note should be made here stating that the amount of litigation that exists in a society exists in inverse relation to a common culture. You will notice that in primitive societies there is very little formal law because there is common law. Disputes are handled through other channels. We live in a litigious society. It is a measure of our impatience. It is a measure of our eagerness to find some consensus that we all acknowledge does not exist anymore or at least does not exist as it once did, and we are anxious about where this situation will lead.)

A polarized community

One of the consequences of the situation in Gaston County was that it polarized the community. Not only did a dispute among neighbors become a highly political dispute, but people who actually knew each other could no longer see each other as loyal opponents, as citizens who happen to have different opinions. They began to see each other as enemies. In our moment of history there is in fact a very real danger that the most basic category of democracy, that of the citizen, will dissolve in the assets of the ideology of difference—exclusive and commensurable difference.

There is a danger that the category of citizen will dissolve in the contention of opposing factions. The problem, of course, is that when we view each other as enemies, we have little recourse but to make war with one another. Citizens, by contrast, are required to engage each other because they have something in common at stake. Citizens disagree, sometimes vehemently, but always in the spirit of loyal opposition. Such a spirit did not exist in Gaston County. Increasingly, with most of these kinds of issues, such a spirit of civility and public agreement about what we have at stake together is disappearing.

A threat to democracy

In sum, when I say that the basic ordering institutions of public life are at stake, I mean that democracy is itself at stake. Power politics is a measure of our inability, our unwillingness, to persuade each other. It is also a measure of the strain that exists upon democratic institutions. Yet, there is another part of the social order that is at stake and is as important as any of the abstractions I have mentioned. I am speaking of the children. In Gaston County, the real losers were the children. It seems to me that this is a cost too high to pay.

When dealing with historical, sociological forces over which we have little, if any, control, what do we do? There is historical momentum we cannot stop. We feel the angst of our moment and rarely give articulation to it. And when we do, it is often in slogans or in cliches. Everyone is running scared, but conferences like this generally provide opportunities to think rationally and collectively about constructive ways to deal with it.

James Davison Hunter

Chapter 6

Moral Education
and American Pluralism

How is it that modern societies stay together? How do they hang together without falling apart?

This is certainly a question as relevant today as it has ever been in the history of our nation. In the context of contemporary America, the question might be put this way: How do we explain the paradox of our national motto, *"E Pluribus Unum"*? At the heart of this paradox is the dilemma of "difference."

In terms of the social and historical context, I believe that we in the United States are in a time of transformation. This is the kind of transformation that will only be seen clearly in a century or two. It manifests itself in what one might call the "dilemma of difference." At first glance, it seems the *pluribus* (the many) in America operates as a healthy political pluralism, but upon closer inspection, intensifying fragmentation becomes apparent. The problem is that fragmentation quite naturally and quickly leads to polarization. Similarly, the *unum* (the unity) is not as healthy as we would like to think. The *unum* still exists culturally and politically, but it is thinning out. We do have some public consensus, but it is largely a consensus without content. Many Americans will say that they believe in justice and freedom, but when asked to define what is meant by such terms it becomes evident that there is little agreement. At best, there is a rhetorical consensus with many Americans imputing fundamentally different and oftentimes contradictory meanings to those consensual ideals. As a result, very often people (primarily elites and activists) have relied on public policy and law to force solutions to societal conflict. How does a modern society like ours hold together? Increasingly, it would seem, through power politics. The activists reason that if only they could get their people onto the Supreme Court, in Congress, and in the state legislatures, onto the local boards of education, and so on, all of our problems would disappear.

This, of course, is not the only answer. There is a pedagogical strategy as well. My concern here is with how the institution of public education in recent times has tried to deal with the dilemma of difference. As the dilemma of difference intensifies, as the paradox of *E Pluribus Unum* becomes increasingly knotty, the answer that education has put forth demands scrutiny. In short, schools have tried to deal with the dilemma of difference through *inclusiveness*. The quest for inclusiveness has moved along different and yet overlapping tracks. The first track is found within the history of moral education, in the explicit effort to cultivate moral understanding and moral character among young people in the schools' charge. The second track, related to and overlapping the first, is found in the history of civics education. Let us look briefly at both.

Moral education

Education, certainly in the Puritan period, was nothing but moral education. The effort to teach students was in fact a catechetical endeavor. Education as moral education was more specifically biblical education. As such, it consisted of memorization of the Catechism and Scripture. Education was institutionalized primarily within the family and only secondarily reinforced by the church. There were relatively few schools in Puritan New England, and those that existed operated primarily through the church.

What I want to emphasize is how the nature of education has changed since the colonial period. First of all, over the past several hundred years the locus of moral authority has shifted from a transcendent God to the institutions of the natural order and the scientific paradigms that sustain them (as envisioned by the Enlightenment Project), to the rational choices of individual subjects. Institutionally, the *sources* of moral authority have also changed, from the institutions and codes of the community of which a person was a part (again mainly defined by family and church) to the sovereign individual. The *content* of moral instruction has changed from the objective moral truths of divine Scriptures to the conventions of a democratic society and now to the subjective values of individual persons. Likewise, the *character* of moral education has changed from the cultivation of shame through the memorization of sacred texts to the rational deliberation over competing values. Not least in all of this, the *premise* of moral education has altered quite dramatically; the sense that children, with all of their endearments, are sinful and rebellious has given way to a sense today that they are by nature good, needing only the proper nurturing and encouragement. Implicit within this transformation is an evolution of the very purpose of moral instruction, from mastery over the soul to the training of character to the exploration and cultivation of the personality.

Underlying all of these changes is a narrative surrounding this question: How is it possible to provide moral education for the young in an increasingly diverse social situation, one that at the same time protects dissent? In every generation, including the Puritan generations, moral education has sought to be inclusive and, even more than that, universal. Yet without fail, any consensus that has been achieved in response to this question is soon attacked for being narrow, sectarian, and ultimately noninclusive. In turn, a more inclusive solution is sought and, once achieved, the process then repeats itself. When the colonial ministers demanded a moral education that was rooted in religion, they in fact meant the particular, dominant doctrines of Puritanism. Recognizing the sectarian quality of Puritanism in the new republic, reformers in the early nineteenth century sought to expand the foundation of moral education to the universal truths of Christianity. Here, too, universal Christianity often took shape as the particular doctrines of a non-denominational evangelical Protestant faith—much to the chagrin of the new and expanding Catholic population. In response, a more cosmopolitan solution was sought in what Horace Mann called a "non-sectarian liberal Christianity." Yet this version too had the sectarian markings of rationalism, Unitarianism, and transcendentalism. It was not long before Mann was rightly accused of a sectarianism of his own. As one of his critics stated, "Everything is sectarianism with him, except what squares exactly with the notions of Universalists and those who have been absurdly called 'pan deists' and 'theo-philanthropists.' Teach one jot of truth more and you are a sectarian, and you shall lose your school, or your school shall lose its proportion of the public funds for education. What is this but to establish by law that Universalism shall be the State religion, taught by public authority, to the exclusion of the views of evangelical dissenters of every name?"

Another of Mann's chief critics put it this way: "It is proper to keep dogmatic theology out of school, but let it be kept out on both sides, the dogmatism of unbelief as well as the dogmatism of belief."

John Dewey's reforms at the end of the nineteenth century and the first several decades of the twentieth century were still further attempts to find a more inclusive and cosmopolitan solution to the dilemma of difference. For Dewey, moral education should reflect a common faith, but for him such a faith was in fact a naturalist moral philosophy that would emerge from the workings of the democratic community—from life together, not from a transcendent entity or a historic tradition. This model of character education has also been battered by the accusation of ethnocentrism. In turn, Dewey's model evolved further toward a more refined blend of secular rationalism, psychological pragmatism, and liberal individualism. All of these philosophical orientations are reflected in different ways in theories ranging from Kohlberg's developmentalism to Rath's values clarification.

Yet the paradox remains unchanged from the beginning. Against the urgent demand made in every generation for a common moral education are the questions:

How can moral education be handled in a way that satisfies everyone? What are the moral parameters of its pedagogy? Who defines its principles? How shall these principles be taught, and by whom? By what authority and reasoning shall these principles be grounded?

Every effort to find a solution that is both effective and inoffensive has eventually fallen apart by revealing its own particularity.

Civics education

Beginning in the first couple of decades of the twentieth century, a second notion of education, civics education, became popular. With the great influx of Germans, Irish Italians, Poles, and other Eastern Europeans at the turn of the century, the problem of immigration presented a dilemma for public education (which was becoming increasingly mandatory throughout the first two decades of the twentieth century). The pedagogy that was first established to deal with this problem was very simply called Americanization. The goal of Americanization was not only to acknowledge and celebrate national differences but also to integrate these differences within a dominant set of American characteristics. In this way, while they encouraged children to keep their native languages and customs, schools mandated that English, the language of their citizenship, become their primary language. Furthermore, civics education also emphasized common American traits and values in the classroom, such as individualism and industriousness as well as a kind of social egalitarianism (owing in large part to the absence of a landed aristocracy).

Through a good part of the twentieth century, policy regarding civics education remained more or less Americanist in flavor. There was a movement that developed during the mid-century called "intercultural civics education," but it really formed a kind of prelude to what we now know of as "multiculturalism." Here I would like to emphasize the difference between multicultural policy and multicultural pedagogy.

Multiculturalism as pedagogy is based upon the rejection of Americanism and Americanization. It is an attempt to recognize, accentuate, and celebrate group differences in history, culture, and experience. Pedagogically, the goal of multiculturalism is to get young people to experience different cultures than their own and to teach them not to pass judgment on different ways of life and different understandings of the world, but to accept other cultures as different but equal and certainly worthy of respect. It is the culture of esteem that unifies us in our differences.

Assessing the quest for inclusiveness

Clearly, more can be said about all of these things. The central question is: What can be said about this quest for inclusiveness, both within moral education and in civics education? In civics education, my conclusion is that the quest has been misplaced; in moral education, my conclusion is that the quest has failed. In both cases, there are unintended consequences that are very problematic.

Take, for example, multiculturalism. The main problem with multiculturalism is that multicultural pedagogy as it is presently articulated operates with a *weak* view of culture. Multiculturalistic pedagogy tends to reduce culture to lifestyle, or to experience, or perhaps to custom. Such trivialization reduces culture ultimately to individual preference and choice. In other words, culture is individualized and psychologized. Children are taught that culture is reducible to values that one can take on or put off at will. Thus, the logic of multiculturalism tells children that, "Yes, there are differences. There are different family structures and there are different religions and there are different food tastes and aesthetic standards. But the fact is that they all function the same way; they all respond to the universal needs of all human beings." By trivializing culture in this way, by operating with such a weak notion of culture, multiculturalist education relativizes culture, ultimately undermining the authority of culture.

Another key aspect of multiculturalistic pedagogy as it is presently articulated is the central concern of its moral agenda: that is, the necessity to build the self-esteem of young people, to make people proud of their roots and, at the same time, gain the respect of other people. Such goals are laudable, and yet they have unintended consequences. One of them is that, in the name of celebrating difference, difference is ultimately washed out and homogenized. I am fond of saying that if the Harvard Law School, which celebrates its diversity of students and faculty—men, women, Hispanics, African Americans, Native Americans, Anglo-Saxons, gays, lesbians, and straights—truly wanted diversity, they would also hire a Mormon or an Islamic Fundamentalist. The truth of the matter is that when you go to Harvard Law School, in spite of all the diversity that exists there, everyone looks at the world in exactly the same way.

I do not want to trivialize the differences to which multiculturalism is generally pointing. However, while such differences are significant, they are not cultural differences of the deepest kind. At the heart of culture is the Latin root *cultus*. The word suggests a cult-like commitment to a certain world view. In this way, culture is not reducible to choice or even to values. In the final analysis, culture is made up of commanding truths, the reality of which are so certain, so authoritative, that to question them is ultimately to question reality itself—this is a strong view of culture! The deeper differences that are underneath the differences of race, class, and public policy that confront us today are for the most part ignored.

That is why, for example, from a multiculturalist perspective we do not deal adequately with the differences that really underlie the problem of abortion. It is difficult to celebrate the kind of differences implicit in the argument over this issue. Indeed, when one views a person who holds the opposite view as basically un-American, it is difficult to find anything to celebrate. The same can be said of homosexuality and, in my opinion, such is true regarding the deeper differences surrounding race and class.

The deeper differences in all deeply divisive issues are largely ignored today. The net effect is that, in the name of celebrating differences, difference is washed out, homogenized, and ultimately passed over.

Regarding the matter of civics education, multicultural education is, in my opinion, absolutely essential for a democratic society and for our schools. Yet it does not nearly go far enough.

Subjectivism

With regard to moral education, the quest has led ultimately to a subjectivism. The prevailing moral education builds its pedagogy upon a framework of moral understanding that is overwhelmingly psychologistic. All of the major players in the realm of moral education, from Dewey on, have been psychologists—every single one of them. This includes William Glasser, Carl Rogers, Abraham Maslow, and Lawrence Kohlberg.

As a result, the pedagogy of moral education ultimately passes on to children a cosmology that is a-historical, heedless to the distinctions of the historical moment and historical forces at play. That is, this pedagogy fails to incorporate any sustained reflection about the nature and impact of character-forming institutions such as the family, youth organizations, and churches.

At the same time, the strategy is almost completely oblivious to the moral influence of deeply embedded cultural ideals and motivations, even taboos, except as they inhibit individual self-expression and psychological maturation. The therapeutic pedagogues, both in theory and in practice, portray the moral life of children in a vacuum. Disembodied moral understandings acquired by faceless children, growing up, or to use the antiseptic cant of developmental psychology, "going through the stages of moral development," for all practical purposes without real families, real schools, real media influences, real peer groups, real synagogues and churches and the like. The portrait is of children, indeed of us all, living outside of history, culture, and the complexity of the social world. What does this mean? It means that there is, within the framework of this strategy of moral education, no possibility of a commitment that goes beyond subjective choice. There is no possibility of an obligation that exists antecedent to choice. There is no possibility of a framework for making sense of commitments that come by, for example, being raised within a particular tradition, or being part of a social stratum.

What I am talking about are constitutive attachments to the community, to family, to other people, to moral traditions that exist prior to choice, that are indeed constitutive of one's identity.

Likewise, any conception of good or evil bound up in the contours of an individual's identity is ruled out from the start. In this cosmology, the moral agent is alone, unconstrained, unencumbered, radically self-governing. The Self is both the source of all moral sensibility and the final object of moral accountability. The dominant moral lesson that has been taught to children, quite apart from any particular lessons that are taught, is to be respectful and tolerant, as autonomous agents. In other words, benevolence, compassion, and justice—all of these things—reside innately within each of us; they simply need to be coaxed out.

There is a big debate within the moral education establishment whether the foundations of those innate sensibilities are rational or affective—mind or emotion. But in the end, all of the theorists of the psychological, or therapeutic, strategy share the conviction that, in the final analysis, moral reality is a subjective reality, that moral authority is a subjective authority, and that moral norms are ultimately the aggregate of subjective sensibilities. Unencumbered by any prior obligations, commitments, and relationships, the person is capable of creating out of no other resources other than his or her mind and emotions the moral justifications to which he or she is committed.

In this way, the psychological or therapeutic strategy of moral education may be set up to oppose certain kinds of behaviors like the use of drugs, the use of violence, cheating, sexual promiscuity, and stealing, but there is nothing intrinsic to the strategy that leads to these ends. So, too, the strategy may be set up to promote other behaviors and attitudes such as achievement, fidelity, compassion, and tolerance; but again, there is nothing intrinsic to the strategy that leads to these ends. The moral ends that are chosen are conceived of as extensions of an autonomous Self; yet these ideas are themselves subordinate to the Self. Clearly the proponents of this therapeutic strategy of moral education, both theorists and practitioners, are well meaning. The ideals such as justice, compassion, and respect are invoked sincerely and earnestly, and yet their view of the Self as a moral agent, as the beginning and the end of the moral life, cannot sustain such ideals.

Conclusions

Let me conclude with these thoughts. First, it seems to me that the results of multiculturalism as presently manifested in civics education, which is an attempt to deal with the dilemma of difference, and in moral education, which in its contemporary manifestation is a therapeutic form of moral education, though well intended, are ultimately tragic.

With regards to the multiculturalism of civics education, "sameness" is ultimately triumphant. For in the name of celebrating difference, we trivialize our differences. Again, I am not impugning the motives of anyone involved. The motives are on target; the ideals, in my opinion, are essential; but the pedagogy itself, as it is presently articulated, does not go far enough.

Within the realm of moral education there is a similar tragic irony. It seems to me that we fail to take differences seriously. In the name of instilling moral character, we actually undermine the very possibility of it being formed.

In a democratic society, particularly one that is being strained at the seams, where consensus grows thinner and thinner in the face of intense social fragmentation and political polarization, the task is not to avoid differences but to take them for what they are with absolute seriousness. I believe that there is no way to get beyond the culture war, in any democratic and just sense, except to go through it. This brings us to the messy, tedious, and often frustrating work of sorting out the details of the struggles, hoping to find within our differences some points of a working commonality.

It seems to me, at a practical level, our first step is to make the distinction between political inclusiveness and cultural inclusiveness. Within a democracy, political inclusiveness is bedrock. It is absolutely essential. Within the concept of political inclusiveness is the concept of citizenship, where we are all equal under the law. I am much more reticent about a strategy of cultural inclusiveness, particularly to the extent—whether it is in civics education or moral education—that it leads to our inability to make any moral judgments. I, like many of you, have an increasing number of students who say, "Gee, whiz, well, you know, the Nazis were a product of their culture. I mean, who am I to say that what they did was wrong?"

As an educator, I want to be able to say, "The Nazis were wrong, and they were wrong for these reasons." I want to be able to say that our policy toward Native Americans was wrong. I want to be able to say that our policy toward African Americans, in so many different ways, was wrong. Moral education, as it is presently articulated, undermines our ability to make those essential judgments. We can only criticize that which violates someone's self-esteem or individual rights.

We have a very difficult time talking about what is "evil." We can discuss what is good, virtuous, and courageous, but to declare something evil is almost impossible within the kind of moral and philosophical presuppositions under which our pedagogy operates today. Political inclusiveness is essential. Cultural inclusiveness, to the extent that it makes us unable to make any real moral judgments, is problematic. The bottom line is, to make moral judgments you have to operate within a realm of particularity, and particularity ultimately is exclusive, and it offends.

But it seems to me that the measure of tolerance in a democracy is not indifference, which is how most of my students would view it. The measure of tolerance in a democracy is the ability to first understand someone so well that you really do disagree with them and yet you will still live with them, work with them, and cooperate with them, finding ways to work together. This, it seems to me, is the measure of a principled pluralism, a principled toleration.

Motivation
for Learning

Dr. Ronald M. Latanision
Professor of Materials Science
and Engineering
Chairman, Council on Primary
and Secondary Education
Massachusetts Institute of Technology
Cambridge, Massachusetts

Dr. Ronald Latanision received a B.S. degree in metallurgy in 1964 from Pennsylvania State University and a Ph.D. in metallugical engineering in 1968 from Ohio State University.

His research at the Massachusetts Institute of Technology focuses on the chemical properties of engineering materials.

He is a member of the National Academy of Engineering and a member-elect of the American Academy of Arts and Sciences.

In 1992, Dr. Latanision served as an adviser on education in the presidential campaign of Paul Tsongas.

Ronald M. Latanision

Chapter 7

An Engineer's Perspective
on K-12 Education

I arrived yesterday just ten minutes before your bus left for the evening event, the boat trip. In manufacturing there's a principle called "just-in-time." That's sort of living my principles, and it's reassuring to see that it works even when I don't try very hard. I did enjoy the interaction with those who were on *The Boat,* but I discovered in those conversations that MIT has something of an image problem. So I thought I would set the record straight in terms of what MIT is all about.

Research universities like MIT actually do have an image, and that image is of being kind of "nerdy"; we're considered to be the nerds of the academic community. That's not always a friendly description, and I leave it to you to determine whether you think the MIT community is truly nerdy.

Celebrate academic achievement

What does nerdy mean? It often means (and I think MIT is a good demonstration) that people are kind of brainy but remote. We sort of feel guilty as charged. No one tries to hide the fact that MIT kids are bright. In fact at MIT we celebrate academic achievement: The average SAT scores are approaching 1500. We celebrate academic achievement not only in our Nobel Prizes and our academy members, but in other ways as well. In fact, in some respects, we celebrate academic achievement literally by poking fun at ourselves. A "Nerd Crossing" sign appeared on Massachusetts Avenue at the main walkway to the main campus from the student residence end of the campus.

Celebrating academic excellence often takes some different forms. The great dome at MIT is a campus landmark. It's about

120 feet high and if you walk near the MIT campus, the dome is the most visible and striking piece of architecture. Every couple of months we find that our undergraduate "hackers" do their thing. This group is unidentified. No one will admit to being a hacker, but everybody on campus applauds the academic and intellectual achievement that hackers demonstrate.

Here is one example. One morning I was driving to work and listening to the broadcast of the traffic report. These folks were absolutely ecstatic when they said, "At MIT there is a police cruiser on top of the great dome, lights turned on and rotating, and there is, it appears to us from the ground, an officer sitting in the car, and he has donuts and coffee!"

That was true except, of course, the officer was a dummy. Now the achievement in all of this is getting that police cruiser up on top of that roof without anyone noticing it. Our physical plant people had to remove it because no one would take credit for it. The hackers provided directions on how to dismantle the thing and bring it down. It was not a ton-and-a-half vehicle. It was actually just a frame on which the fenders and so on were mounted. But it was a wonderful accomplishment. And it's just one of a number of things that these kids actually have done.

You know that the Harvard-Yale games symbolize a big rivalry and, not being Ivy Leaguers, we feel a little bit put out. So a couple years ago during the Harvard-Yale game, it appeared that the turf on the floor of Harvard stadium was beginning to deteriorate. Then, within a matter of seconds a weather balloon actually mushroomed from the turf. Of course it interrupted the game. You had to have been there to see the looks on the faces of the referees and the people in the stands and the football players. When it reached full size, the balloon exploded.

The headline in the next *The Tech,* the MIT school paper, was, "MIT 1, Harvard-Yale 0."

We felt that was, once again, a wonderful engineering accomplishment. It was a weather balloon, planted clandestinely and inflated remotely from outside of the stadium. A spotter in the stadium sent a signal to his colleagues when to launch it. We didn't want to hurt anyone, we just wanted to make a point. And it did.

One last item. If you've ever visited Boston and walked across the bridge that connects the Cambridge side of the Charles River to the Boston side, you will notice that the bridge is calibrated in units called "smoots." It turns out that somewhere back in the 1950s, at one of the fraternity parties, there was a thought that it would be good to calibrate this bridge. It happened that there was a relatively short and I guess very popular gentleman whose name was Smoot. So these fellows thought: what better way to calibrate the bridge than in smoots?

The trick was to convince Mr. Smoot to lie down on the bridge. He did. He then was rotated systematically. It turned out the length of the bridge was exactly 364.4 smoots and one ear.

This bridge, like many other bridges in the United States, eventually was in great need of repair, so about five or six years ago the Department of Public Works in Massachusetts actually removed the deck, replacing it with new materials.

It became pretty clear that the bridge would have to be recalibrated. And, as good fortune would have it, a younger member of the Smoot family was at MIT, and the bridge was recalibrated in about 1990 in exactly the same way. It turns out the junior Smoot was almost exactly the same height as the elder Smoot.

An intense learning environment

I'm poking a little bit of fun at what we do at MIT, but it's a very intense environment. In fact, the students like to describe an MIT education as something like a drink from a fire hose. That's pretty close. There are about 4,000 undergraduates, each class about 1,000. And there are something like 7,000 graduate students. In our freshman class, nearly 40 percent of the students are women. Does that surprise you? The usual image of MIT is essentially of a male-dominated—a *white* male-dominated—institution. In fact, when I began teaching there twenty years ago, that was a fact. Probably not more than 4 or 5 percent of the freshman class were women. Now about one-third of our undergraduates are Asian Americans. And 17 percent of our students are minorities—about

7 percent African American, about 7 percent Hispanic, about 3 percent Native American. That's not just by accident. About ten years ago, we made a conscious decision at MIT to begin the process of changing the demographics of our student admissions so that, ultimately, our students will be representative of the United States, at least in terms of demographics.

In addition to engineering and science, which is what we are best known for, we have Pulitzer Prize–winning composers on our campus. John Harbison is a Pulitzer Prize–winning composer of music. We have best-selling authors, both fiction and non-fiction. In fact, a couple of years ago, Alan Lightman's *Einstein's Dream* and Lester Thurow's *Head to Head* were both on the New York Times' bestseller list at the same time, a first for MIT. We also have an MIT student symphony that plays in Lincoln Center and Kennedy Center. We like to claim (and I think this is true) that we have the second largest number of men's and women's NCAA athletic teams of any university in the country. Football actually has had a long history at MIT. But there was about a 70- or 80-year gap in which we did not play football. About ten years ago, we resurrected football and, after a couple of seasons, the football team was invited to some post-season bowl games. But the MIT team decided not to go because the bowl game coincided exactly with our final exam period.

We have a school of engineering, a school of science, of architecture, and urban planning, of humanities, and the Sloan School of Management. We do not have a school of education. But we do have a program at MIT which certifies undergraduates to teach in a public school. There are about forty enrolled in this program, which is a small number, but it's as large or larger than some academic departments at MIT. And we have the seed for a school of education and maybe, in the not too distant future, that seed will begin to blossom into something that I hope will be a twenty-first century school of education.

I wanted you to hear this because I think it's a perspective that will give you an indication of where I'm coming from as an engineer, for I want to give you an engineer's perspective on K-12 education. I think there are some things we've learned in the last five or six years that may be of some value.

From a coal-mining region

Let me tell you a little bit about myself, to put some perspective on this. I grew up in northeast Pennsylvania, in the coal mine region near Scranton. I went to a one-room school for the first four years. There were six grades on the first floor and six grades on the second floor. The elementary school and high school were all in one building. There were only four or five chairs in each grade, for that was the number of children. There were about a hundred families in town. While I was in school, several small rural schools were consolidated into a larger school, so instead of having four or five in my class, there were thirty-nine in my graduating class.

I went back to a high school class reunion a few years ago and, while talking with some of my classmates, we began to recognize that when we were growing up, there were no adult males in our community. They had died in coal mines. My father died at age 45 of what today would be called "black lung." My oldest brother died at 27 in a mine accident. We were all raised by our mothers and our siblings.

Motivation is key

I think that's a very important observation because my sense is that motivation is one of the most important elements in education—in anybody's education. You've got to have something that motivates you to learn, to want to learn, to want to make change. Change is difficult, but I was really motivated. I was convinced that I did not want to be a coal miner. But there weren't many options. My mother worked in a parachute factory. The only other industry in northeast Pennsylvania was textiles. Coal miners, if they were laid off in the coal mines, would absolutely not work in a textile mill. My father would never have even considered doing that.

The fact is, none of the three boys and two girls in our family would have gone to college on the strength of our family wealth. My mother raised our family on a $35 per week paycheck. However, like many first- and second-generation descendants of immigrants, we looked at education as a way to leave the coal mines. My brother went off to Lehigh University and got a degree in mining engineering. My father was dead set against that. He just didn't think college educations were necessary. My mother was the visionary. She insisted that we all get college educations, one way or another.

Without having the resources, I could have, I guess, convinced myself that I just never would go to college. I could have said, "Well, I'm going to do what everyone else has done for generations and go into the coal mines." But that thought was enough to convince me to work hard enough to get some scholarship help. So I went off to Penn State and got my bachelor's degree in metallurgical engineering. It's kind of close to the mining industry because you do mine metallic ores in order to produce metal, so I guess my roots were not totally severed.

After four years at Penn State, I crossed the border to Ohio and got my doctorate in metallurgy at Ohio State. I spent the next six years in industry. I worked as a post-doctoral student at the National Bureau of Standards in Washington, and spent four-and-one-half years in the research center of Martin Marietta Corporation. This was a good experience because it put engineering into practice.

I joined the faculty at MIT about twenty years ago. Along the way, the educational process had become important to me, though frankly, when I was hired at MIT no one ever asked me if I could teach. At a research university (I don't know whether our administrators would admit to this), the reality is that we're hired because of our research interests, though we all teach. In fact, at MIT we have about 1,000 faculty and 4,000 undergraduates, a very interesting ratio. We pay a lot of attention to teaching, especially undergraduate teaching. I guess I've always had it in the back of my mind, given my background and going to a one-room school, that teaching was number one. I'm telling you all these things because I believe there are a number of items in my experiences that actually bear on some of the problems we are dealing with today in the education of young people.

Education has two major purposes

My sense is that an educational system ought to serve at least two major purposes. It ought to allow youngsters to reach their intellectual potential. And, in a broad sense, it should provide the means by which young people are prepared to take a place in society. That may be very simplistic, and it may not be your vision of what education is, but just indulge me for a moment, and let's assume my view is at least a reasonable approximation of what an educational system might deliver. It might allow someone to reach their intellectual potential and at the same time allow them to become prepared to enter a society that, increasingly, is a technologically intense society.

If we take that as being a goal of education, then I would submit that our educational system today is not serving those purposes well. I want to emphasize the word *system*. The educational system is not just people like yourselves who are administrators or teachers. I don't just mean K-12 or whatever. I mean the whole system, the educational system K-99. Given the social importance of education, the educational system involves everyone in our society, whether you're a parent or a teacher or a businessman or a legislator or a newspaper reporter. The fact is that we're all part of this educational system.

Engineers are trained to think about systems, but usually about systems that are much less complex. I think it was far easier to develop a system to get a man to the moon and back than it is to try to change an educational system with such complex social, economic, political, and cultural implications. Yet I think there are indications that the system needs to be changed. What I'd like to talk to you about is my perspective on what kinds of issues are susceptible to change and are important to change.

A root-cause analysis of education

Let me tell you what symptoms concern me. I will put this in the context of what engineers like to talk about as a "root-cause analysis." If an aircraft engine, which is a system, fails, we instruct our students to perform a root-cause analysis on the failure of that engine in order to determine what caused the system to fail. Then, based on that diagnosis, they must determine what sort of remedial action to take.

Let's suppose there is an engine failure. The question is, Why did it fail. What are the possibilities? When you look at it afterwards, what you'll see is essentially a cylinder-like vessel full of bits and pieces of turbine blades and disks. Why did the engine fail? For example, it may be that there was a defect in one of the components. The Sioux City, Iowa, DC10 crash several years ago was that type of incident. Or an engine may have ingested birds in flight. That happens. It may be that there was a fuel problem. There are a number of possible causes. What's important to determine is what happened so you can determine how to improve the operation of that engine or know that no operational change is necessary.

If an engine ingests a flock of birds, it's not a failure of the design or metallurgy of the engine; it's just an unfortunate reality that this does happen. Here I will add a footnote. When an engine manufacturer designs jet engines, there are a number of standard tests. One of those tests is called the Standard Two-Pounder. In this test, chickens, roughly two pounds in weight, are fired from something like a cannon into an operating jet engine in such a mass that if the engine has been designed properly and is operating successfully, it will ingest those chickens without a hiccup. The idea is that if you're in flight and you're landing at Newark airport and happen to ingest a flock of seagulls, you don't want the seagulls to actually shut down an engine. So you design a test and consider what would be representative of a flock of birds and use that as part of the testing. This test is really crucial. Development of engines has been delayed sometimes for long periods of time because they could not pass this Standard Two-Pounder test.

In England, the commission that develops trains used the Standard Two-Pounder to test the windshields on new trains being developed for use in the tunnel under the English Channel. What they discovered was that these birds were just smashing the daylights out of their windshields. So they sent a letter off to the FAA [Federal Aeronautics Administration] in the United States, describing their procedure, and asked for some advice. The FAA sent back three words: "Thaw the chickens."

Symptoms of a failing system

Now let me apply a root-cause analysis to the failures I see in primary and secondary education. During my twenty years at MIT, particularly the last four or five years while chairing a council at MIT on primary and secondary education, we have focused a great deal of energy on this issue. I'm not sure we're right, but we're working hard at it. So let me tell you what I see as symptoms of this failure.

As I understand it, something like 20 percent of our high school students drop out of school. In urban population centers that number is higher—sometimes multiples of that. Many who graduate from high school leave with fifth-grade skills in reading and math. Fifteen percent of the population in the United States is functionally illiterate. In terms of a science and math education, only about 20 percent of our high school population will ever take a chemistry course if they have a choice. Physics is an even smaller fraction, more like 10 percent. There are many reasons for these figures, but I'm not going to go into the reasons. I'm telling you what I see as the symptoms of a failing educational system.

American industry spends something on the order of $40 billion per year in training programs. Many of these are remedial programs which address this fifth-grade reading and math skill issue. In universities our retention rates, especially in science and engineering, are declining.

Now on top of this is a matter addressed in a 1990 report entitled *Report of the Commission on Skills of the American Work Force,* chaired and edited by Ira Magaziner, who then found his way into the Clinton White House. This report pointed out that by the year 2000, 70 percent of the jobs in America will not require a college education. On the face of that, that sounds not too troublesome, for if you were to look nationally, only about one-third of the people who leave our high schools enter college. In fact, given the retention rates, less than a third who start college will actually end up with a college degree. So the commission's finding is not really incompatible with what we know is true of our culture today.

The problem is that the majority of those who are not college bound will not have the kinds of skills that employers need. At least that's what I'm seeing. I use as a reference a wonderful book, *Teaching the New Basic Skills,* by Richard Murnane from the Harvard Graduate School of Education, and Frank Levy from the Department of Urban Studies at MIT. They spent eight years doing the research and writing. The "new basic skills" are in sharp contrast to my father's skills as a coal miner. My father had a fifth-grade education; my mother went to about the third grade. My father could easily mine coal. He had to show up dependably on the job. He had to be physically fit. But he didn't have to have writing skills or computer skills.

Three types of skills

Levy and Murnane describe three skills as important: hard skills, soft skills, and computational skills. By hard skills they mean math and reading ability, at least at a ninth-grade level, and some ability to look at a problem and work it. They describe as soft skills the capacity to work in a team, as part of a group, and the capacity to communicate orally and in writing. The third element, what they describe as "computational skills," basically means the capacity to do word processing and, even more interesting, the lack of fear to take on some new software. This is what employers are telling them are the kinds of skills that employers would like to see in people entering their work force, including entry-level jobs.

The people who leave high school and enter MIT obviously have most of those skills. They certainly have the hard skills, and they have computer skills, for these kids grow up with computers. But I'm not so sure the kids who are entering MIT would make good employees if they went directly into the workforce because the communication skills of students today are diminished from what those skills were twenty years ago, based on the freshmen entering MIT twenty years ago. In fact, it looks to me as if (and this is only my observation) that these kids are very comfortable at a computer keyboard, but if you ask them to write a paragraph, they have a hard time. The faculty and administration at MIT recognize this, and we have instituted a communications requirement for all undergraduates. Not only must they take courses in science and math and chemistry and physics and some courses in humanities, but they also have to meet the standards we set for a communications requirement, which includes both written and oral expression. That is partly because of the feedback we've gotten from the people who have left MIT. Scientists and engineers, in general, have never been great writers, but there's absolutely no question that if you're going to function as an engineer, you've got to be able to communicate. You've got to be able to write your reports and express your thoughts and ideas. So this to us has become a very important part of our students' educational experience.

Let me just point out what Murnane and Levy have concluded about the notion of these new basic skills. If you look into the demographics, you will find there is a disparity in salaries between the youngsters who enter the workforce directly from high school and youngsters who have gone to college and then enter the workforce. The conclusion you come to is that a college education is something that we ought to make available to every American if we want them to have livable wages. President Clinton has taken that flag and, as you know, this is an important element in his administration, and the Department of Education is intending to provide tax benefits and other forms of relief so that all Americans can get a college education.

However, what Levy and Murnane have concluded, and what I have felt for a long time, is that not everyone needs to go to college. That may sound heretical, especially coming from a university professor, but I believe that. Why is it that there is a salary disparity? Is it truly because people have learned something in college that is more valuable to employers? That is the conclusion you might come to first.

What Murnane and Levy found is that employers are hiring college graduates not so much because they've been in college for four years but because the employers believe that during those four years they developed basic skills that our high schools are not providing kids. Not that high schools couldn't provide that experience, but how many schools offer speaking and writing courses?

What about computation? If I look into a high school today and compare it to the experience I had in high school, it looks like a marvel to me. There are computers and technology of all kinds in many schools. Schools look like they're capable of providing experiences that I never had when I was growing up.

The reality is that employers are saying something different. Employers are saying that the capacity for education is there, but it's not being exercised.

Consider this: In order to get a job on a manufacturing line at Ford Motor Company, people need ninth-grade reading and math skills. The national average is something like fifth-grade reading and math skills. If you don't have the required ninth-grade reading and math skills, then you're unemployable. That fact should serve as some sort of motivation, but too often it doesn't.

There is something in the realities of American education that I would describe as being almost a tragedy. I'm referring to the youngsters in vocational schools. In vocational schools a lot of the skills that I've been talking about are more likely to appear than they are at some mainstream schools. But vocational education is perceived in the United States as being a second-class experience. Maybe that perception, in some ways, is justified. But the reality is that it's also become something of a self-fulfilling prophecy. If you say it often enough, people begin to believe that they don't want to send their kids to a vocational school. There's no reason why youngsters going to a vocational school could not be prepared to enter the workforce or to go to college or both if they choose. There is a cultural issue here that makes vocational schools less appealing.

But if I were a 14-year-old today and thinking about what I might do in the future, there are vocational schools I've visited during the last five years that I would die to go to. They have core educational programs that look very much like a university in terms of core math, science, and even reading and speaking skills. They also focus on technologies, such as electromechanical systems, things that an engineer would resonate with. I often describe MIT as being something like a "super voc tech." That may be a little bit of a stretch, but I believe that every university has to have a vocational character.

Virtually everyone who enters our educational system will ultimately find their way into the workforce for some part of their lives. Whether you talk about kids entering the workforce directly from high school or with an intermediate stop in a college, almost everyone has to work somewhere in their lifetime. This is an important point.

An analysis of symptoms

I've given you a sense of my reading of the symptoms. It's now time to perform something of a root-cause analysis on these symptoms. I've identified dropout rates and the fact that people are underachieving. It's not that there isn't instruction available. No, in many cases the kids are just underachieving. Why?

Is it, for example, that our standards are too low? Is that the problem? Is it that we need to change our curriculum? Should we have a better curriculum? Are school days too short? Are school years too short? Are teachers under-prepared? Are schools managed poorly? Are unions a problem? These are things you hear, and maybe in each case there are issues we would want to address. You can make the case that our standards ought to be raised. But, on the other hand, if you've already set standards and kids are underachieving, does raising the bar even further make it more likely that they're going to achieve more?

Frankly, all of those issues deserve attention and, as far as I can tell, every one of the issues and others have been on various agendas. If you go to an NSTA [National Science Teachers Association] meeting, or any teachers' meetings, you will hear all these items discussed.

Attitudes

I would like to make the case that the fundamental issue is attitudes. By attitudes I mean many things. It may mean motivation that people have been given. It may mean convincing people that education is relevant. It may mean a feeling of self-worth among youngsters. It may have to do with our values. I put all of those under the major flag of attitudes.

Let me describe what I mean. First, I find among students (obviously not every youngster) that achievement is not central to their culture. Let me give you a couple of examples. These are just anecdotal. Over the last six years, I have visited schools in affluent communities and schools in inner cities that are not so affluent. I often discover that kids in affluent schools look at me and see this academic nerd, and they actually come to the conclusion that they don't want to be nerdy. It's not just provoked by my presence. I've had kids tell me: "It's not cool to be smart." It may be cool to be a good athlete, it may be cool to be other things, but it's not cool to be smart. I think this is particularly a problem with women and with minorities.

We had an interesting experience at MIT a couple of years ago. I mentioned the fact that 40 percent of our undergraduates today are women. We had a television crew from one of the local television stations in Boston come over to MIT and they interviewed Sheila Widnall, one of the associate provosts. She's now the secretary of the Air Force, but she was associate provost at that point. They asked Sheila if she would identify a group of young women who could be interviewed about education. One of the young women she chose was a blonde. The reporter asked these kids about their experience, why they had come to MIT, what their experience had been. This young woman pointed out that when she was in high school and thinking about applying to universities, she talked to a guidance counselor. Her interest was in Cal Tech and MIT and a couple of other research universities. She told the reporter that her guidance counselor looked her square in the eye and said, "Look, you're just a dumb blonde. Don't bother applying to those places." Well, this kid applied to MIT and was admitted. She was studying aeronautics as her undergraduate major. Clearly, she's got all of the academic credentials of an MIT undergraduate.

Our president, Chuck Vest, saw the interview and for the next couple of months, in his speeches, would talk about this and point out that the student may be blonde, but she is not dumb. This kid is a rocket scientist.

I have a daughter, a graduate student in microbiology, who tells me the peer pressure on kids not to be bright, not to appear to be smart, is real.

Underachievement

At the other end of the economic spectrum there are similar pressures. I've talked to young people in some of the Boston public schools who remind me of myself at the same age. Remember, I came from a family in which there was very little income. I could not have gone to college if I had had to depend on my family to pay the tuition. There are kids today who are economically deprived and who will take the position that there is absolutely no way they will ever have the means to go anywhere to college, let alone to an MIT. This sense of despair feeds an attitude of: "Why should I bother working hard in school?"

The tragedy of that is it's not accurate. At MIT we fight very hard to maintain our essentially needs-blind admissions. Basically we tell youngsters that if they've got the academic credentials, we'll find a way for them to come to MIT. I think most universities now have much the same attitude. But there is that misunderstanding, and it breeds underachievement.

This is a part of our culture, but it's not universal. In the city of Lowell, Massachusetts, there is a very interesting phenomenon occurring. There is in Lowell a very large Cambodian population. The regeneration of an old mill town has led to jobs that have attracted immigrants and a substantial Cambodian population. If you go into the Lowell school system and talk to teachers there, you know what I'm going to say. The reality is that you've got seventh-, eighth-, ninth-, and tenth-generation American students in those schools with first-generation Cambodian refugee children. If you ask the teachers who are the stars in their classes, they're not the ninth- and tenth-generation Americans; they're the Cambodians. These kids are still hungry to learn. They look at that opportunity as a means of getting to something better than what they have. Most have just learned English. Their parents don't speak English. This sounds like an echo to me as I watch all of this. I could speak to my parents, but I couldn't speak to my grandparents.

Cambodian families pay a lot of attention to education. Talk about peer pressure. It may not be cool in some segments of our population to be smart, but in Cambodian families, it's just the opposite. There's still an expectation on the part of the families of these young people that they're going to have to work hard to develop their educational experiences. And they do. They're exposed to the same textbooks, the same teachers, the same buildings, the same facilities as the tenth-generation Americans, and they're achieving. Why can't the other kids?

Motivation for some, not others

I think that, at least in part, it has something to do with the attitudes or the motivation. Maybe they don't see the relevance in education. The thought of being a coal miner convinced me. That was relevant to me. That was real motivation. Maybe the same thing happens with the immigrant families of today.

There is an organization called The Center for Talented Youth (CTY) at Johns Hopkins. Every year we host a program at MIT on

material science as part of the Saturday sessions that CTY orga-
nizes. In the opening session one year, I said how glad I was to see
them (about 500 parents and children were attending) because we
at MIT celebrate achievement. I said they obviously were achievers
or they wouldn't be there. I told them the same thing I've told
you, that I don't think academic achievement is central to our culture for young people in the United States.

I said, by contrast, that when I travel in Japan my sense is that
achievement is really, truly central to the Japanese culture. I used
as an example what I've seen in Japanese taxis. In the United States,
being a taxi driver is probably a job of last resort. It's not a job you
seek; it's something you do if you don't have any alternatives. But
in Japan, Japanese taxis are impeccable. They're clean. The drivers
are dressed in jackets or nice clothes. They drive their cabs with
white gloves on. When the cabs are not being driven, these fellows
typically stand outside the cab and, using something like feather
dusters, they clean the car. In a Japanese restaurant, the service is
polite, almost too polite. Take a sip of water and before you know
it, somebody's filling your glass. Your coffee never gets cool. The
taxi drivers and waiters are always trying to be efficient. I actually
think the attitude is: "If I'm going to be a taxi driver or a waiter,
I'm going to be the best taxi driver or waiter I can be."

That's what I hear. My Japanese colleagues tell me that is part
of their culture, their work ethic. So I made this comment in this
room of achievers, and I asked, "How many of you have been to
Japan and what have you noticed about Japanese taxi drivers?"

I expected that in this audience of parents and kids, somebody would stand up and say the Japanese really work hard at
driving taxis or something like that. But instead some youngster,
probably a seventh-grader who had obviously been to Japan, stood
up in the back of the room and said, "In Japan, they speak English." This kid broke up the whole audience. His answer was not
what I had expected, but he was right. Now think about that. It's
true. It may not be true in Grand Rapids or Holland, but if you
come to Boston or Washington and get into a taxi, you're lucky if

you find a cab driver who speaks English. Most don't. It is a job of last resort.

The attitude of parents

I also want to comment on the attitude of parents. One of these high-achieving kids said, "You know, parents have attitudes, too." I like the way kids express things; they put it right to you.

My wife is a painter, and when I go to an opening of one of her shows and someone asks what I do, I like to be sort of contrary about it. I simply say, "I'm a teacher." What happens usually is that the person just sort of disappears; they're gone. When I say that I teach at MIT, that usually attracts them. There's a certain value attached to teaching, but only under certain circumstances.

What I find ironic is that there is this public attitude that teachers are among the underachievers in our population. There is that old line that if a teacher could do something else, she or he would. The irony is that people with this attitude are trusting the minds and the education of their children to this group of under-achievers.

When I reflect on my experience in school, the teachers I re-member best are women. There were lots of very good women teach-ers in my school system. Maybe that was part of the demographics in that area because of the coal mines and the death or illness of men.

Today, young women have many other options that provide both more community respect and more respectable incomes. They have options; they can become engineers or scientists or whatever they choose. I think there is a very important message in the fact that there are MIT undergraduates who actually want to teach in the public schools. They're not underachievers; these kids are seri-ous students.

I have met teachers I consider to be world-class educators. I have also met some I consider to be misplaced. I don't know what that mix is. You know better than I do, given your role as adminis-trators, how many of your teachers you really would like to keep and how many you would rather not keep.

But the reality is that there is a mix. And if we want to make teaching respectable, we've got to get parents back on line and we've got to change this community attitude, this parental attitude that teachers are really underachievers.

Community attitudes

Finally, I think there are community attitudes—not just kids or parents, but the whole community. I sense that in the United States we have lost the sense of community. The common good is often sacrificed to our own special interests. If you look in Washington, you can see that very clearly. But I think it's something that has crept into American life. We are a nation of 250 million special interests, and not many of us are willing to look at the common needs as closely as we should. I'll give you just one or two examples that I think make the point.

In Massachusetts we have a law called Proposition 2°. It's like California's Proposition 13 regarding the real estate tax base. Proposition 2° in Massachusetts says that real estate will not be taxed at more than 2° percent of its full value and, moreover, that communities may not raise the real estate tax more than 2° percent every year. One exception is that a community may override Proposition 2° if the residents feel there is a good reason and if voters agree to it in a referendum. In a Massachusetts city a couple years ago, there were two items up for a vote. One of those had to do with trash collection. The city decided it needed to buy more trash-collecting hardware—machines and trucks. The second had to do with making some improvements on school buildings. You know which one passed, hands down. A majority voted to buy new trash-collecting equipment. The referendum on school building repairs got voted down. There are lots of issues involved with this, but the simple interpretation is that everybody has trash, not everybody has kids in school.

That's how people vote, and I think that states are now beginning to respond to this. I understand that in Michigan, for example, you no longer depend on the real estate tax base for your school funding, that it is now based on sales tax.

In 1993 Massachusetts passed an education reform act which requires, as one of its elements, foundation level support for education, which means that every school in Massachusetts receives a $5,500 allocation for every student. That's important because we had tremendous inequities, for if you base revenue for school systems on real estate, it guarantees inequities. In Massachusetts, in places like Fall River and New Bedford, which are old fishing communities, the towns were spending something like $2,500 per year per student. In Wellesley and Weston, it was more like $12,000 a year for each student. No question that Weston offered kids more in terms of facilities and instruction and opportunities than New Bedford. This is beginning to change, and it's a very good thing.

Your attitude and motivation

Attitudes play a key role in education. Attitudes shape what motivates you. Attitudes provide some relevance in terms of education. Attitudes help you to understand why you ought to study computers or know something about writing or be able to read a manual at work.

The question is: What can we do about addressing this matter of attitudes? How do we respond to these issues? If I'm in an engineering classroom and I'm talking to someone about the root-cause analysis on an engine failure, we don't stop with the analysis. We don't stop just because we found the problem. We have to then decide how to fix the problem.

We've now performed an engineer's root-cause analysis on the failures of the educational system. We've narrowed the cause of that failure to attitude—the attitudes of the community, the attitudes of teachers, and the attitudes of parents and students.

What can we do about it?

A lot, in this engineer's view. But that's the topic for my next talk.

Ronald M. Latanision

Chapter 8

An Agenda to Engage
Research Universities
in K-12 Education

The two operative words in terms of increasing student achievement are motivation and relevance.

I'll treat this as an economist might in terms of a supply-side and a demand-side approach. On the supply side, we have kids who are underachieving. I want to be clear that my goal when I talk about underachieving is not (despite my inclinations as an engineer and a technologist) to convert everyone in our educational systems to the mindset that they ought to grow up to be scientists and engineers. In fact in the United States today there are only about 2 to 3 percent of the population who are practicing scientists or engineers. It's a relatively small fraction, though it is larger than the fraction of the population in the United States involved in agriculture. And with the strength of our agricultural capacity, we not only serve our own agricultural needs but much of the rest of the world's needs. The same is true in many respects of our science and engineering enterprise.

I want to stress that my goal here is not just science literacy, it's really what I would describe as technical literacy. I consider science to be value-free, not value-less. I mean that in this context: it is only when we begin to apply what we have learned about nature that we have to make value judgments.

On the other hand, science is often counter-intuitive. And this comes to the issue of relevance. Science is counter-intuitive in many cases, and this is something a practitioner has to understand in great depth. But to the average person on the street, if you wanted to talk about what it means to be literate, I don't think that means necessarily understanding all of the abstraction that's typical of science or engineering. I think that's very important for practitioners to understand. If the goal is technical literacy for the broad population—and in my mind that's what the goal should be—I think everyone ought to understand that in our culture and in the industrialized world, and on much of this planet, technology actually pervades our lives. There is, as James Hunter pointed out, perhaps a historical mindset that technological advance and economic growth coincide. I don't think that's always true. There are cases where technology does, as it always should, serve society. But there are also lots of examples where technology has been more of a disservice to society. Those are the kinds of judgments that we have to make; it is part of what is involved in the judgment and decision-making that a technologically literate society should do. We haven't done that all that well in the United States. But technology does pervade all our lives: in communication, transportation, health care, and waste treatment. It's hard to imagine anything about our lives in which technology has not entered and is not intimately involved. And so I think it is important that we ought, in considering what it means to be literate, to consider not only the capacity to read and write and perform some mathematics at appropriate levels but to understand how technology impacts and affects our lives. In that instance the fundamental issues are once again motivation and relevance.

The demand side

What about the demand side of this equation? I take the demand side to be very simple, actually. On the one hand I think everyone in this country will at some point enter the workforce. For some of us there will be this intermediate stop at a university, but ultimately we will enter the workforce. Therefore I would choose, for the sake of discussion, to describe the demand side as being made up of two components: the university and industry.

It's interesting to me that in terms of that equation, if you are interested in pursuing a university education, you have to meet admissions requirements. Just to personalize this a little bit, if I think back to my own education, I would never have had the credentials to enter MIT as a freshman. I went to a school, as I told you yesterday, in which there were 39 people in my graduation class. I was lucky to have algebra, let alone calculus. No way did I have the credentials to enter MIT. I was fortunate in being able to find my way to a wonderful state university, Penn State. But the point I'm making is that universities have admission standards. And they say, "Look, if you don't meet this standard, I'm sorry. We can't admit you." It simply says that universities recognize that in order to make decisions on who should be enrolled, standards are used in our admissions process. Frankly, I would have been like a fish out of water at MIT as a freshman. It was hard at Penn State, given where I was starting from. But to enter the sort of intense learning environment that's typical of MIT as a freshman with my qualifications would have been a disaster. So I don't think there's anything wrong with setting admissions standards and drawing lines and saying yes and no.

What's interesting to me is that from the point of view of an engineer, and from the point of view of one whose students often go off to industry, what I see in my discussions with people in industry is that there are no equivalent standards to enter industry. A diploma is really not perceived by people in industry as a suitable demonstration of the development of skills required on a job site, whether it's a service job or a manufacturing job. I described yesterday some of the skills that people like my colleague Frank Levy and Dick Murnane from Harvard consider to be relevant skills from the point of view of people entering the workforce. Actually, the same set of skills is useful to college freshmen as well.

There are attempts to correct this. In Massachusetts, the State Department of Education has adopted, as part of the 1993 Education Reform Act, a system of decision points. For example, in tenth grade there will be implemented in the coming years a high stakes exam which will determine whether a youngster has the competency to proceed through eleventh and twelfth grades. That's a high stakes exam. If people don't pass it, they will repeat. Obviously there are going to be many, many unhappy people because, if you look at the standards that are being established, I would say that a large fraction of our young people are not going to meet the standards that we're setting. That will create some awkwardness, no question. There is also a proposed Certificate of Mastery; the architecture of that certificate is still being developed. The Certificate of Mastery is intended to demonstrate that a youngster has the capacity of going on and handling college-level courses. There is also a Certificate of Occupational Proficiency, this for the large fraction of the youngsters in Massachusetts who choose to go into the work force directly from high school. (This doesn't diminish the potential that they may sometime go to the university.) Having a Certificate of Occupational Proficiency is one way for the state bureaucracy to provide credentials.

On the face of it, it sounds very good, and perhaps some of it is good. But in terms of the issue of the Certificate of Occupational Proficiency, we still have a dilemma: by and large the decisions on what credentials are required in order to meet that certificate are being generated by people in the Department of Education without much input on the part of the beneficiaries of that certificate, namely the employers. That's a flaw, and so the question is, What kinds of credentials do employers want?

I think Murnane and Levy have answered that pretty well. They're saying, from their research in industry, that there's a set of skills that are required: hard skills, soft skills, and computational skills. The hard skills are math and reading proficiency at a ninth-grade level, problem-solving capacity, and so on. Soft skills are skills that have to do with working in groups and team-related matters. Plus communications—a capacity for communicating in writing and orally.

Those skills are not typically stressed in a mainstream high school or a vocational school. So there is a disconnect. I'm sure this will change, in Massachusetts at least, because there's now a sensitivity. But that's the point I want to make. Employers are clearly beneficiaries of the educational system. And if we are sensitive to their needs, we will hopefully establish metrics in which they have had some input. If we don't do that, then I think we will continue to hear, as I do today, from both service sector and manufacturing sector employers, that young people leaving our school systems don't have the credentials that they're looking for. So I think it's very important, in terms of an agenda that addresses these issues, that we are sensitive to the beneficiaries of the product of this system. Of course, employers are just one beneficiary, but an important one.

Let me talk a bit about what that agenda might look like, both from the point of view of the industrial needs I've described and an agenda that involves the academy, both as educational statesmen and even more pragmatically in terms of being an ally to educational change in the United States. I think universities have the potential to be a real obstacle unless they become genuinely involved. The current discussion of involving industry and education is at least one current manifestation of the concept of "school-to-work," though some are more comfortable describing it as "school-to-career." Some consider implicitly that school-to-work is for people who will not go to university, but will directly enter the workforce. School-to-career takes into account the reality that a youngster may in fact have an intermediate stop at the university before entering the workforce. But the general theme is that eventually everybody will find, at some point in their lives, that they have to work—maybe not for all of the useful years, but for a lot of them, and for many of us that's pretty full time.

"Work-based learning" may be an even better term than school-to-career. At the university level we have established internship programs and co-op programs which take young students at the undergraduate level to job sites where they have real-world experience in terms of what it means to be a chemical engineer, or a material scientist, or an electrical engineer. Thus the content they receive in the academic courses is supplemented by some experience in the world of work. That has been enormously successful at the university level, though I'm talking about a relatively small fraction of the people. My point is that we know at the university level that this is a successful and useful part of the experience of undergraduates. Now, not all undergraduates do that, though many do. In fact, at MIT a large fraction of our undergraduates have some sort of co-op or industrial experience before they leave MIT.

School-to-career

School-to-career from the point of view of the establishment in Washington is, in my judgment, in need of a great reality check. The thinking is that high school students ought to have, during their junior year, experience working on a job site. If you think about that, it means something on the order of four or five million kids. What I have found in my discussions with people in industry, and this includes CEOs and research managers and others, is reluctance to have young people at that age on their job sites for a number of reasons. Liability emerges, given the litigious nature of contemporary society, as a major issue. It can be dealt with, but it's still an issue. There are other issues. Many American companies have downsized. What does that mean? What are the implications for school-to-work? First, there's an image problem. If on the one hand you're laying off senior engineers and you're bringing sixteen-year-olds onto the job site, even though you know they're not going to replace engineers, it does create an image problem. Even more important is the attitude that "If I have agreed to bring in young people and give them a meaningful experience while they're on the job site, I'm going to have to take time away from an engineering staff which is now reduced in number." So school-to-work seems to me to be a very unworkable program in the broad sense.

There is absolutely no doubt that there are examples where school-to-work has been very successfully applied, but they typically involve very small numbers of kids, and they're very costly programs.

There's a wonderful program in Boston called Protech in which young people get experience in medical care and health care. It's been in existence for something like thirty years, so it precedes school-to-work by a long way. It's very expensive and provides a wonderful experience, but it's hard to imagine how you would extrapolate that to four million people, and that's where the rub is.

Nevertheless, having workbase experience in some fashion, even in the classroom, does provide youngsters with some guidance that helps to address the question of relevance. You begin to understand why it's important to study math or why it's important to be able to read instruction manuals. That's not a fifth-grade reading ability, it's at least ninth-grade. We're concerned that a lot of kids leaving our schools can't read instruction manuals. School-to-work does provide a certain degree of relevance in terms of why young people should study and learn and work hard at learning. It may even provide some motivation because ultimately they recognize why it's important to work hard at education and to achieve their potential.

I think work-based learning programs will be successful only if industry has a voice in establishing the metric that determines whether kids have achieved at a sufficient level, and if industry really puts some teeth into this recognition. This may sound Draconian, but I would like industry to tell people that if you don't meet these standards, you're unemployable. Maybe that's too harsh, but if motivation means that kind of approach, I'm willing to endorse it.

Industry's role in education

Over the years I've been trying to understand the motivation on the part of industry to get involved in education, and there are a lot of industrialists who are concerned about education.

This has taken many forms, some of which have been spectacularly unsuccessful, in my view. They've adopted schools, they've provided fiscal resources, but when you get right down to it, there would be an admission, if people were honest, that a lot of what industrial organizations have done has been more driven by public relations than by a real sense of commitment to educational change. That's not exactly a good thing, though it does provide some degree of visibility for the company, and it indicates the company's concern.

I think we'd have been a lot further ahead today if some of the resources that were distributed very broadly were focused on some critical mass effort. I don't think a public-relations approach is very effective.

In Massachusetts, without the involvement of the industrial and business community, there would (1) never have been an Education Reform Act and (2) there would not be the policing of that Education Reform Act that there is today.

The Education Reform bill was literally written by a group of people in an organization called the Massachusetts Business Alliance for Education—a handful of business leaders who were committed to this. They've held the legislature accountable for implementing what has been put into law, including such things as foundation-level per-capita support for the education of kids. The legislature, interestingly enough, would have backed down in the first year after that bill was passed had the business folks not applied pressure. Being a beneficiary, industry has a role to play, and in the best of circumstances it exercises that role.

A university's role in K-12

Let me turn to the other side of that demand equation, namely the universities. Let me first put some context into this. A few years ago, in 1995, we invited the leadership of the National Academy of Science, the Institute of Medicine, the American Academy of the Arts and Sciences, and the National Academy of Engineering, along with serious academics and some from the foundations, about fifteen people, to look at the question: What role could research universities play in K-12 education that would build on their strengths and at the same time allow the research universities to play the role of an objective participant?

We ended up with an agenda that was remarkable. There were only five items. This white paper led to additional meetings in which MIT President Chuck Vest and Neil Rudenstine, his counterpart from Harvard, participated. They then encouraged their colleagues from four other universities, Michigan, Stanford, Texas, and Wisconsin, to join them in signing a letter which was sent to

Neal Pings, president of the Association of American Universities (AAU). The AAU is an association of the more than sixty universities in the country.

The letter essentially said, "There are a number of issues that have been identified as being common to all of our universities. They are concerns in which we have to begin to act. We would like to suggest that the AAU institutions begin looking seriously at addressing these issues."

This letter was not trivial in terms of having it written and signed. To get six presidents to agree to a letter was quite a marvel to watch. But it did get signed and sent, and I think it represents a milestone in terms of a commitment on the part of the senior administrators at six major institutions to encourage their colleagues to begin looking in a very statesman-like way at issues that are important at all of their institutions.

Undergraduate core courses

One of the issues has to do with core teaching at the university level. Now, what does that have to do with K-12? At MIT, freshmen have to take, as part of their undergraduate core, a set of courses before they begin taking the courses in their major. They are required to take courses in chemistry, physics, and biology, which is actually a new requirement at MIT. There is also a math requirement, humanities requirement, and a developing communications requirement, which has to do with writing and public speaking.

The interesting thing about our core courses is that none of them are taught in a way that would be entirely compatible, I think, with the kinds of changes that are being recommended for high school science and math. I'm sure many of you have had experience with the NCTM, the National Council of the Teachers of Mathematics, standards or the new National Research Council science education standards that were published by the NRC just about two years ago. You will realize that they are oriented toward experiential learning and inquiry-based instruction, though not at the expense of content. It's intended that youngsters will understand principles but would be able to problem-solve and apply what they learn. So the approach involves both content and process.

At American universities, and I can tell you only about those I've had experience with—Penn State, Ohio State, and now at MIT—that is not typically the way we teach our science core. Clearly there are people who are majors who will take upper-level courses and there will be a lot of abstractness and inquiry in these courses. But I'm talking about the undergraduate core.

What is the role of the core curriculum at a university? I believe that it should be to provide our undergraduates with a sense of literacy. We don't expect every undergraduate to become a biologist or a chemist, but we do expect them to be literate in terms of biology and chemistry and math and physics. This tells us that this is something that we need to look at, because what we see in the not too distant future is a potential disconnect between what will constitute (based on such things as the National Research Council science standards) a good high school science education and what kids are going to see when they enter the freshman year in terms of core teaching.

I should also mention that at MIT, and I'm sure this is true of other universities, my MIT colleagues who are in the arts have pointed out to me repeatedly over the last five years that what scientists are beginning to discover is what teachers of the arts have known for a long time: You learn by experience. You don't learn to dance by reading a textbook. Or paint, or act. Of course there is some of that, but you learn by practicing, by essentially experiential means. I think they're right. I have a wife who is an artist, and she reminds me of that constantly. Experiential learning can be a very real way of learning. The danger about experiential learning is that it seems to be content-free. There are a lot of people who are very concerned that all we're going to do is make kids feel happy and warm and that they really will go away not having learned a whole lot. I think that danger is real, but it can be managed if, in fact, both content and process are involved in experiential learning. That is what I see happening.

Admissions standards

Core teaching at the university level is one issue. Admissions policies are another issue. If you are the parent of youngsters who you hope will go on to the university, you expect that your youngsters are being exposed to science and math education that meets the standards that have evolved. Further, you trust that when they apply for admission, they're going to be assessed and examined and tested on the basis of that approach rather than an approach which is foreign to them. The parents have a point there. Today's approach, particularly through SATs and ACTs, is much more oriented toward word association and facts. Unless there is an alignment between what's happening in K-12 science and math and our admissions policies, then once again there will be a disconnect. And I think it behooves us as institutions of higher learning to deal with that issue now instead of in a fire-fighting mode, which is likely to happen if we don't take it on and deal with it in a very reasoned way. So this is on the agenda of the items that have been described in this college presidents' initiative that has been spearheaded by the six presidents I mentioned.

Teacher preparation

The third issue is teacher preparation. I mentioned to you that at MIT we don't have a school of education, but we do prepare youngsters to teach in the public schools. Our teacher-education program has been designed basically on the strength of the wishes of young MIT undergraduates to have access to the kinds of skills and experiences that are required to go off into the public schools and teach. Those skills include such things as childhood cognitive development. We do teach such courses at MIT, so that's one we can handle. There are other kinds of things they need to learn, like classroom management. Classroom management is something we don't typically have in our curriculum. But we do have an alliance with Wellesley College, which does have a school of education, so we do exchange programs. Some of their students take our courses in educational technology, and some of our students take their courses in classroom management. The net result is that we do certify undergraduates from MIT to teach in the public schools.

You should be sitting there saying, "Why would anyone go to MIT and spend that much money if their goal is to go out into the workforce where the average starting salary is probably as much as one year's tuition?" That was a real concern to us. We've tried to manage that in the following sense. We're very fortunate that our alumni have been among our most active and effective supporters in developing these initiatives at MIT. It turns out that many years ago, the class of 1950 developed an endowed fund, and the fund was intended to provide scholarship aid and loan forgiveness financial arrangements for the progeny of the class. The members of the class of 1950 are now having grandchildren, and so they're at a stage where they were willing to consider making that endowed fund available to the undergraduates who are actually enrolled in our teacher certification program. That takes some of the sting out of paying tuition bills. And I will remind you that about two-thirds of the MIT undergraduates receive financial aid. Their parents aren't footing the whole bill. So in fact what we're doing is using some of our resources to actually subsidize the preparation of teachers.

Those are the three items the presidents identified. There are a couple of others that some of us had encouraged them to consider, but they did not at this stage. I just want to mention two others. One has to do with faculty incentives. At MIT I chair a Council on Primary and Secondary Education. Its members include faculty, staff, and students, so it's an institute-wide committee that has all the segments of our population involved. But no junior faculty are involved in this council. The reason is simple. In terms of the currency of academic life at MIT and other research universities, when you talk about promotion and tenure, what counts most is publications and your research credentials and teaching to a certain extent, not involvement with something that today is outside of the traditional mission of research universities, such as the K-12 education. So we haven't involved junior faculty.

Secondly, I have heard from some of my senior faculty

colleagues on the council and elsewhere that their involvement in K-12 activities, at least at the onset, was treated by department heads in such a way that they were actually penalized rather than rewarded. In other words, it was not perceived by a department head as being something that really served the department's interests. That's a pretty serious issue. To address it requires that senior administrators send a signal which says that this is a reasonable and important activity for our faculty to be doing. Department heads really do control a lot of the very important issues that relate to promotion, tenure, and salaries, so we would like to see the research universities and the senior administration in particular take on this issue of faculty incentives. I don't think it serves our purpose to discourage people who are interested in educational issues, and by interested I don't mean abandoning our research interest, but adding to the kinds of things we do. Universities do expect such service from their faculty, not only to the institution but outside of the institution. My hope is that these kinds of activities will become acceptable in terms of the culture of research universities as examples of the kind of service that a faculty member might provide. But that does take some commitment on the part of senior administrators.

The final issue has to do with public awareness. Maybe the broader issue is the issue of public will. I think universities can serve as the objective spokesman or statesman if we take on that battle. It's important that someone, some entity, some body, begin to function in that way. Frankly, I can't imagine that we can actually make the kinds of changes that I've talked about in terms of inspiring student achievement, motivating kids, and providing the kinds of relevance that I'm describing without the support of the public and, particularly, parents. As administrators you must have a hard time making a significant change in your school system unless you get parental support.

Resistance to change

There are many elements of resistance to change. From the point of view of the student, if it isn't relevant, why should I study it? If you can't respond to that argument, you're not going to convince kids that they ought to take chemistry courses even if they're experiential in character. They've got to want to learn. If there isn't alignment between admissions standards and the changes that are being proposed and implemented, particularly in science and math education, that's going to represent a significant obstacle to parents who aspire for their children to attend a university.

If you look at every segment of our community, you can imagine where there might be pressure points and obstacles that universities can address. I think the nicest summary of this is a comment from Chuck Vest's predecessor as president of MIT, Paul Gray. A few years ago, Paul really raised the banner in terms of educational activity at MIT when he was interviewed by a reporter from the *Boston Globe*. It was a very wide-ranging interview. In a comment about education he said he thought it a paradox that at the same time that technology is becoming so pervasive in our lives, there is such public disinterest and apathy in terms of science and math education. He said this was a paradox that he didn't understand and didn't know how to deal with, though he thought it was real and therefore a concern.

That comment launched some activities at MIT in this area. I've often been amused by an anecdotal answer provided by the youngster who was asked the question, "Which do you think is worse, ignorance or indifference?" The kid's answer: "I don't know and I don't care." I suppose that's a possible commentary on the paradox that Paul identified.

A sound response to these issues requires public will. People have to want the best education they can find for children. The question that emerges is, "What is it that moves Americans? What is it that really makes change happen in the United States?" There may be many answers, but I think one of the answers is actually something that James Hunter brought up in a different context: It's fear. Maybe threat is a better way of putting it. You think about the galvanizing effect on the American population of the Cuban missile crisis, for example. The threat of a national emergency always galvanizes the public. But this is also true for personal threats, such as the campaign having to do with tobacco and smoking. I don't think I saw anyone in this whole population smoking. If you do, I'm not trying to single you out, but I didn't see very many smokers. Do you remember the television campaign having to do with smoking in the late '70s? They were showing lungs that had been exhumed from people who died after having smoked. That was very compelling. But it was the fear, in that instance, of serious illness as a consequence of something that could be controlled if there was a will to control it. Probably the current manifestation of this public response to threat is the concern that Americans have broadly about diet and dietary issues. There are more people today who talk about cholesterol than probably knew how to pronounce it ten or fifteen years ago. And it's basically because we are concerned about our health.

There's a sense of threat, or maybe urgency, in all of this that is somehow hard to imagine in terms of education—a process that takes twelve years at a minimum, except for those who drop out of the system, and this in itself is a concern. Somehow the urgency is not associated with an educational process. Yet what we do today for the kids entering our kindergartens is going to affect what happens to them twelve years later when they leave high school.

We need to begin to develop and affect the public will. It can be done. It has been done, as I've illustrated, though frankly I don't know how to do it in terms of education.

If the business community—with all of its public-relations and advertising machines—and the universities—as an objective body of interested people—were to become involved, perhaps we could make the case for making our educational system function to the point where students achieve their intellectual potential. Maybe we could make that case compelling enough so that both parents and students would be motivated to make that happen.

I don't know. I have no experience in public relations or advertising. But I have a sense that this is an important part of the agenda of what should happen in the future. And it's something we have in mind to pursue as part of the college presidents' initiative.

Dr. Lisa D. Delpit
Benjamin E. Mays Chair
of Urban Educational Excellence
Department of Educational Policy Studies
Georgia State University
Atlanta, Georgia

Dr. Lisa D. Delpit holds the Benjamin E. Mays Chair of Urban Educational Excellence at Georgia State University. The major focus of her work is finding ways and means to best educate urban students.

Dr. Delpit has studied teaching and learning in multicultural societies in Alaska, Papua New Guinea, and Fiji.

She received a B.S. degree from Antioch College and an Ed.D. from Harvard University.

Dr. Delpit's honors include the Harvard University Graduate School of Education 1993 Alumni Award and the 1994 American Educational Research Association Cattell Award.

Her recent book, *Other People's Children,* has received several awards.

Lisa D. Delpit

Chapter 9

Creating Educational Excellence
for Urban Children

It was not an easy decision to take a position named in honor of the esteemed Benjamin Elijah Mays, nor a position that was previously filled by the esteemed Alonzo Crim. I have, as my mother used to say, "plenty big shoes to fill."

I have discovered in my research on the life of Benjamin E. Mays that when he returned to Atlanta in 1940 from Howard University to become president of Morehouse, his offer was for a $5,000 yearly salary and a house. I must say that Georgia State has been considerably more generous to me, but the house would be nice.

From sharecropper to president

Although there are many who knew and were influenced by the magic of Dr. Mays, there are a significant number who do not know much of the amazing history of this gifted man. Dr. Mays' parents were both born into slavery. They were sharecroppers, very poor but very proud. Benjamin, the youngest of eight children, was born in 1894, ten miles from the town of Ninety-Six, South Carolina. He declared in his autobiography that his earliest memory was of a mob of white men with guns who rode up to his father, cursed him, drew their guns, and made him salute. They made him take off his hat and bow down to them several times, and then rode away. Benjamin was not yet five years old. He later found out that this was one of the mobs associated with the infamous Phoenix Riot, which actually lynched several African Americans on that and subsequent days.

Dr. Mays also states in his biography that his color was never an issue in his family. Both his parents were dark-skinned and the children ranged from black to brown. In his small town, African Americans ranged in skin tone from black to white, but he said that he and his family never felt sorry for themselves because they were dark-skinned. He and his family accepted Africa as the home of their ancestors. To quote his perspective, writing in 1971, he said, "Although I can appreciate the current emphasis on blackness, I'm mighty glad I didn't have to wait 70 years for someone in the late 1960s to teach me to appreciate what I am, BLACK!"

He also adds that despite the fact that the larger society did not agree with her position, his mother constantly told all of her children that they were as good as anybody. Apparently Benjamin took her advice to heart because he went on to acquire a doctorate from the University of Chicago, to teach at Howard, become a dean, and later was named president of Morehouse, where he served for twenty-seven years and brought the college from a mere junior college to one of the premier institutions in the country—black or white. His oft-quoted phrase: " If Morehouse isn't good enough for anybody, then it isn't good enough for Negroes."

A demand for excellence

Dr. Mays was a man who stood for excellence in all he said and did. He demanded it from himself and from his students. He stood for what he believed in, even though in the segregated South to do so meant his life was frequently in danger. He served in many capacities to push for justice and equity and was appointed to many boards and delegations. He turned down at least seventeen much more lucrative offers during his tenure at Morehouse because he was committed to giving it his all.

A vast number of our African-American male leadership today were connected in some way to the work of Benny Mays. He was a mentor for such diverse folk as Lerone Bennett, Jr., Martin Luther King, Jr., Maynard Jackson, Andrew Young, Julian Bond, Alonzo Crim, and countless others. He was consulted by presidents in this country and in others.

After retiring from Morehouse, he went on to take the challenging task of becoming the first black president of Atlanta's Board of Education in 1970, just when Atlanta confronted one of the worst crises in its history: The court had ordered a comprehensive plan for the desegregation of the public schools. Dr. Mays was 75 years old at the time.

Both racial communities were up in arms. White opposition was organized, articulate, and blatantly emotional. Hundreds of teachers allegedly threatened to resign. Mass rallies were held. Dr. Mays was able to bring the city through the crisis, improve education in Atlanta, and then go on and serve for twelve years, not retiring until he was 87 years old. When he retired *again* at 87, he retired to work on three books.

Dr. Mays was a man who was committed to education, to creating opportunities for those who were least well served by the larger educational establishment, to creating, as he said, "not doctors, lawyers, or scientists, but men." He did this for *other people's children* whom he adopted as his own.

I titled my recent book *Other People's Children* because that is whom we in education see every day. There are at least two ways to view other people's children, and I'd like to give you some stories from the two perspectives.

Other people's children

Carolyn is a young Irish-American kindergarten teacher who has been teaching for five years. The school at which she teaches had been a predominantly white, middle-class school in a quiet neighborhood in New England. However, because of recent redistricting, the school population now includes children from a housing project not far away. These children are almost exclusively poor and black. Thus, Carolyn and the other teachers in this school are newly faced with a population of children with whom they are completely unfamiliar.

I'm working on a research project with Carolyn. She asked me to observe a little boy named Anthony, a five-year-old black child from the projects whom she has identified as a child with behavioral, learning, and language problems. She wants to use the results of my observations to "get him help."

In observing Anthony in the classroom, I noticed that he gets no positive feedback during the course of the day, but instead receives a tremendous amount of negative comments. I've taken Anthony out into the hallway several times to talk to him and play with him to get a better assessment of his abilities.

The following dialogue is taken from the transcript of my conference with Carolyn. I'm attempting to point out some of Anthony's positive points.

Lisa: Anthony told me that he liked school and that his favorite thing in the class is group time.

Carolyn: That's amazing since he can't sit still in it. He just says anything sometimes. In the morning he's OK; after nap he's impossible.

Lisa: He's really talking more it seems.

Carolyn: He's probably never allowed to talk at home. He needs communicative experience. I was thinking of referring him to a speech therapist. He probably never even gets to use scissors at home.

Lisa: He told me about his cousin he plays with after school. It seems he really does have things to talk about.

Carolyn: It's unfortunate, but I don't think he even knows what family means. Some of these kids don't know who their cousins are or who their brothers and sisters are.

⁓

Charles is a three-year-old African-American boy who likes a little white girl in his nursery school class. Like most three-year-olds, his affection is expressed as much with hugs as with hits.

One morning, I notice that Charles is hovering around Kelly, his special friend. He grabs her from behind and tries to give her a bear hug. When she protests, the teacher tells him to stop. A short time later, he returns to her table to try to kiss her on the cheek. She protests again and the teacher puts him in "time out."

I comment to the teacher with a smile that Charles certainly seems to have a little crush on Kelly.

She frowns and replies that his behavior is "way out of line." She continues, with disgust in her voice, "Sometimes what he does just looks like lust."

⌒

One evening I received a phone call from Terrance's mother, who was near tears. A single parent, she had to struggle to put her academically talented fourteen-year-old African-American son in a predominantly white private school. As an involved parent, she had spoken to each of his teachers several times during the first few months of school. All of them assured her that "Terrance was doing just fine."

When the first quarter's report cards were issued, she was dismayed to see a report card filled with C's and D's. She immediately went to talk to the teachers. When asked how they could have said he was doing fine when his grades were so low, each of them gave her some version of the same answer: "Why are you so upset? For *him* C's are great. You shouldn't push him so much."

⌒

In each of these stories, the teachers could not see the child for the stereotypes that they held about them. Let me share three quotes from other teachers:

Elizabeth Harris is a teacher of first graders: "God's little flowers. That's what I call them. Every one a little different, but every one so sweet. And just like a garden, the classroom has got to be a place that nurtures them. They don't all need the same thing. One might need a little more sunlight, another a little fertilizer, some might even need a little pruning, and some might need to roam free. They're just so precious that it breaks my heart to see the hurtful way they are treated. Some teachers think that they are hard because they live tough lives, but they are just as fragile as house flowers."

A second teacher, Margaret Rossi: "I can't think of anything any one of my students can do to keep me from teaching them. If more teachers understood the connection between themselves and their students, they might feel the same way. These children are the future. There's no way for me to have a secure future if they don't have one. It's going to take three of them to support one of me in my retirement years. They have to be capable of assuming highly skilled positions. They have the brain power, but they need the opportunity. The society can't keep saying, 'I'm sorry, but there's no place for you.' I'm amazed we don't see more rage among African Americans."

And a third teacher: "They are so smart, but so few teachers recognize it. I'm so afraid they will meet the same fate as last year's class. We worked so hard to get them into algebra, and then they go on to middle school where they are treated like they don't know anything. Last year's students were so bored with the math they had, which was actually arithmetic, that they started cutting math class to come back over here for me to teach them. When I explained that I couldn't teach them, they just stopped going to math class altogether and failed for nonattendance."

These are views of "other people's children." We can either view the poor, urban, often African-American children we teach and their parents as flawed, incapable, dangerous, and pathological. Or we can see them for the brilliant, resilient, delicate, hopeful beings they really are. This is the first step in doing anything about urban education—making sure we see them as the latter.

Urban education

There is much talk about the "problem" of urban education, much talk about research to study the problem, and little belief that we can do anything about it. After all, we can't change the community, can't change the parents, can't change the crime, the drugs, the violence.

But guess what? We can still create excellent education. I know it because it's been done, from Dr. Mays' time to the present.

At the classroom level, Gloria Ladson-Billings, in her book *Dreamkeepers*, writes about eight excellent teachers of African-American students. Some of the teachers are African Americans, some are European Americans, but all are teachers who are committed to children and successful at teaching them.

Successful schools

At the school level, Dr. Asa Hilliard and his colleagues found that there were many successful schools for poor children, but they're not widely known. There are videotapes documenting schools in which poor children received an excellent education.

He found several commonalities in these schools, but not a particular instructional methodology. What he found was school leadership, instructional leadership, staff development, monitoring of students' progress, collective problem-solving, parent involvement, high expectations, productive climate and culture, and a particular effort to make sure that essential skills were taught and learned.

We even have evidence of excellence for poor children at the school district level. Dr. Sherwin Adams was a principal in Dallas, Texas, and succeeded in changing the performance of the worst school in the district to the highest performing school. He did this twice, with two different schools.

Then he took on a school system that was considered the worst in the nation academically, the Benton Harbor Area School District in Benton Harbor, Michigan. The entire predominantly African-American district improved more academically in one year, from 1993 to 1994, than any other school district in the United States. Benton Harbor's 1993–94 scores were higher on the Michigan State test than many of the much more affluent middle-city districts in Michigan. This was accomplished in less than one year.

Adams brought in just three new staff members, so the same people who had worked in the worst school district in the nation now worked in one of the best. Those who watched him work said he set the tone for positive thinking and success. He transmitted his enthusiasm, his belief in the ability of students and staff, and his commitment to hard work. He made schools a place where everyone belonged and everyone excelled.

Nine factors

The point of those stories is that we can provide an excellent education for poor, urban children. It has been done.

There are nine factors that I have found through my own research and from the research and practice of others whom I trust and respect which I believe must be in place in order to successfully educate the children of color that we typically fail. And not just successfully educate, but excellently educate. I'm still developing the list, but I'll share what I've come up with this far.

1. Teach more.

Understand the brilliance of the children who sit in front of us and teach accordingly.

We can't teach less because we are "being nice," which happens all too frequently. In an insightful 1975 study entitled *Racism Without Racists: Institutional Racism in Urban Schools*, Massey, Scott, and Dornbush found that under the pressures of teaching and with all intentions of being nice, teachers had essentially stopped attempting to teach black children. In their words, "We have shown that oppression can arise out of warmth, friendliness, and concern. Paternalism and a lack of challenge have created a distorted system of evaluation in the schools."

This is not a new concept. Certainly Benjamin Mays would have made the same statement as one of his contemporaries, Carter G. Woodson, wrote in 1933 in his book *The Miseducation of the Negro*: "The teaching of arithmetic in the fifth grade in a backyard county in Mississippi should mean one thing in the negro school and a decidedly different thing in the white school. The negro children, as a rule, come from the homes of tenants and peons who have to migrate annually from plantation to plantation looking for light which they have never seen. The children from the homes of white planters and merchants live permanently in the midst of calculations, family budgets, and the like which enables them sometimes to learn more through contact than a negro can acquire in school. *Instead of teaching such children less arithmetic, we must teach them more than white children.*"

2. Demand critical thinking.

It doesn't matter what the curriculum is; it doesn't matter, apparently, what the methodology is. There are all kinds of methodologies that can be used, but whichever one is used, we have to demand that children think. When I was in Alaska doing some interviews with Native-Alaskan teachers, a Native teacher told me that the only Native teacher she ever had in school would do things like leave a broom on the floor in the morning. The kids would come in and step over the broom as they moved to their seats. After everyone had sat down the teacher would say, "Not one of you is thinking. If you don't think, who is going to think for you? Nobody picked up the broom. What is the problem here?" And she continued to push and to push so that those children were always on their toes, always thinking.

One example of a thinking curriculum is the Algebra Project. Bob Moses' focus is teaching all children algebra by the end of middle school, no matter what background they come from. They have to be pushed to think. Many children, if you don't demand thinking until later in their school career, are uncomfortable with the process. School has educated them out of thinking. We cannot give them a choice as to whether or not they are going to think, we must push them to do so. We have to make sure they get that opportunity. Often children who are less successful in school tasks are better at thinking through real-life problems.

3. Provide the emotional ego strength to challenge racist societal views of the incompetence and pathology of children and their families.

One of the things that successful teachers of children of color say to them is, "You *will* learn! I know you will learn because you are brilliant." Jaimie Escalante taught poor *barrio* children in California to pass advanced placement calculus tests. He would say to them, "You *have* to learn math. Math is in your blood. The Mayans discovered zero!"

We have to be able to say to our children that we understand, and you need to understand that this system is set up to guarantee

their failure. To succeed in school is to cheat the system, and we're
going to spend our time cheating. One junior high student working and struggling with math told me, "Black people don't multi-
ply; black people just add and subtract." Here is a child who set
severe limits on her potential based on a misguided notion of the
limits of African Americans, a notion, no doubt, culled from perspectives presented to her from popular media. She had never been
told that Africans created much of what we know as higher math.
She knew none of the great African-American scientists and engineers.

Teachers have an important role to play here. They must not
only make children aware of the brilliance "in their blood" but
they must also help children turn any internalized negative societal view of their competence into a compelling drive to demand
that any system attempting to relegate them to the bottom of society recognizes and celebrates their giftedness.

4. Recognize and build on children's strengths.

To do this requires knowledge of children's out-of-school lives.
One of the teachers in *Dreamkeepers* speaks of having brought candy
to school for a holiday party. She thought she brought enough
candy for all the children, but the candy disappeared before half of
the children had been served. She was perplexed, but then discovered that the children were putting some of the candy in their
pockets. After some inquiries, she realized that they were doing so
in order to take some home for their siblings.

Many teachers might say these children were stealing. They
might say, "I'm not going to bring candy into this classroom anymore because these children are selfish and untrustworthy." But
this teacher understood that what was happening was a real strength
that she could build on, a sense of nurturing that could very well
make peer tutoring or collaborative learning much easier to implement.

When I was a new teacher, Howard was a first grader in my
class. I was ready to take the advice I was given to seek special
education for Howard. I remember particularly that, among other

academic problems, he was having real difficulty with math worksheets. You know the worksheets where there are pictures of five pennies and the child is supposed to indicate that they equal a nickel, or show that four quarters equal a dollar, and so forth. I don't care how much we went over and over those worksheets, Howard just couldn't get it. I visited Howard's home and talked to Howard's mother and his grandmother. I found out that Howard's mother was suffering with substance addiction and that Howard was responsible for getting his four-year-old physically challenged sister up every morning and on the bus to school. He also did the family's wash, which meant that he had to have a lot of knowledge about coins, about money, and he was very good at it. He had to know about money because he knew he couldn't get cheated.

What I found out through that experience was that I, without knowing this child, almost made a terrible mistake. I assumed that because he couldn't do a task in my classroom, a task that was decontextualized and paper-bound, he couldn't do the real-life task it represented.

One of the things that I think is very difficult for our teachers to do, particularly our teachers who may not be from the same cultural background as the children, is to understand where strengths may lie. We must have means to discover what the kids are able to do in church or what kids are able to do on the playground with their peers.

A lot of our kids in urban settings come to us with what we refer to as "street smarts," yet we seldom seem able to connect that kind of knowledge to school problem-solving and advanced thinking.

5. Use familiar metaphors, analogies, and experiences from the children's world in order to connect what children already know to school knowledge.

One teacher taught about the governmental structure of the United States by connecting it to the black church structure. She had the children collect the articles of incorporation of their churches. She then showed how the minister could be compared

to the president, how the deacons could be compared to the legislatures, and how the board could be compared to senators. Not
only did the children learn about the Constitution in a way that
they were able to comprehend with much greater clarity, but they
also learned that institution building was a part of their culture as
well.

Another teacher, Amanda Branscome, who happens to be a
European American, had a class of ninth graders who were considered special education students. She had the children teach her the
rules for writing a rap song. "No, no, you just can't write it, you
have to tell me the rules," she told them. "I know nothing about
rap songs. I've never even heard one. How can I write one?"

So the children had to explore meter, verse, and the structure
of a rap song. After they had done that—and that was a massive
study on its own—she used their rules to show them that
Shakespeare used rules to write his sonnets as well. Then they set
about exploring his rules.

My mother, who was a teacher (I come from a family of teachers), taught plain geometry one year by having the students make
a quilt. There was a student who dropped out of school to get
married and have a baby. The students presented this quilt to this
young woman as a present.

There are several connections here: Obviously by making a
quilt, the students were creating something for someone they cared
about. But they also used the theorems of geometry to decide how
to piece the quilt together. School knowledge was connected to a
sense of community.

Teachers really are the arbiters of knowledge, the cultural bro-
kers who connect the familiar to the unknown. We have to help
our teachers learn to do that.

6. Create a sense of family and caring.

Jackie Irvine, a friend and colleague at Emory University, interviewed a teacher identified as an excellent teacher and asked,
"How do you view teaching? How do you ensure children's success?"

The teacher answered, "Well, the first thing I have to do is make the children mine." She said that on the first day of school she goes down each row and says, "Son, what is your name?" The little boy would say, "My name is Justin Williams." And she'd say, "No, darling, in this class your name is Justin Williams Brandon." She'd ask the next child, "Darling, what's your name?" "My name is Mary Johnson." She'd say, "No, sweetheart, in this class your name is Mary Johnson Brandon." If you haven't figured it out yet, the teacher's last name was Brandon, and she proceeded down each row to give each child her last name. She then said, "Now you are all my children, and I have the smartest children in the entire world. So you are going to learn more this year than anybody ever learned in one year. And we are going to get started right now."

In her dissertation research, one of our former graduate students, Dr. Madge Willis, looked at a very successful school in Atlanta and found an overwhelming sense of family, a sense of connectedness, a sense of caring. I have discovered that children of color, particularly African-American but not limited to just African-American, seem especially sensitive to their relationship between themselves and their teacher. I've written elsewhere that it appears that they not only learn *from* a teacher but *for* a teacher. If they don't feel connected to a teacher on an emotional level, then they won't learn, they won't put out the effort.

Barbara Shade writes, "African-American children value the social aspects of an environment to a greater extent than 'mainstream' children, and tend to put an emphasis on feelings, acceptance, and emotional closeness." Shade contends that, "African-American interpretations of the environment determine the amount of time and kind of effort students will spend on classroom tasks."

I was made particularly aware of that cultural phenomena when I worked at Morgan State University, a historically black institution. The amount and kind of effort the custodial staff put in was very much directly related to how they felt about the person who asked them to do it. And that is a phenomenon that any of you who have ever been in predominantly African-American settings understand. The level of perceived connectedness is directly related to the level of effort that we tend, as a people, to expend. We place an extremely strong value on personal connections. Dr. Mays, during his tenure as president of Morehouse, got to know every single one of the students at Morehouse. Each one was invited to his house for dinner at some point before graduating.

7. Monitor and assess children's needs and then address them with a wealth of diverse strategies.

The particular words in that statement are important. We do a lot of *monitoring* and *assessing*, but we do less *addressing* needs in the larger school system. We administer tests and then we don't seem to do anything with the results except to test more. Until someone can prove that we can fix a broken arm with more X-rays, I think we need to rethink our testing practice.

In order to monitor and assess the needs of children who may come from a different cultural background, the notion of basic skills almost needs to be turned on its head. We must constantly be aware that children come to school with different kinds of knowledge. Our instruction must be geared toward understanding that knowledge, building on it, and teaching that which children don't already know.

In order to offer appropriate instruction, we need to understand that what we typically think of as *basic* skills are those skills that middle-class children learn before they come to school: knowledge of letter names and perhaps sounds, color names, counting, recognition of numerals, familiarity with storybooks and with particular kinds of language found in them. We also believe that critical and creative thinking, the ability to analyze, the ability to make comparisons and judgments are higher order skills.

It is often the case, however, that for children who are poor, critical thinking skills are *basic*. Those are the skills they come to us with. They are accustomed to being more independent. Often they are familiar with real-life problems and how to solve them. But they are sometimes not familiar with what the *school* calls basic skills.

Those children who appear to quickly learn the basic skills presented in school typically learn most of them during their five or six years at home. Children who did not learn these skills at home, and do not learn them in the first five or six months of school, are often labeled as *too street wise* by adults who see their ability to solve problems with near adult sophistication as violating some preconceived notion of childhood innocence.

An Anglo teacher I worked with in Atlanta successfully taught Native children in rural villages in Alaska. When she came to the city to teach more middle-class children, she was appalled at how dependent the middle-class children were. "They don't even know how to tie their shoes," she said of her kindergarten class.

The village kindergartners not only could tie their shoes, they could fix meals for their siblings, clean up, and help their parents with all sorts of tasks. They took on the responsibility of keeping areas of the room in order with little adult supervision, which freed Bonnie to work on academic tasks.

She found the city kids unprepared for such responsibilities.

What I am suggesting is that we teach traditional school knowledge to those children for whom basic skills are not so basic, and appreciate and make use of the higher order knowledge that they bring with them. On the other hand, I suggest that we appreciate the school knowledge middle-class children bring and teach them the problem-solving and independence that they sometimes lack. Then middle-class children will know what to do when the paint spills other than to stand in the middle of the floor and cry.

Middle-class parents transmit school knowledge so naturally that they do it without even being conscious of what they're doing. While progressive teachers rail against any type of direct teaching methods, they seldom realize that that is in part exactly what middle-class parents are so good at.

When my own daughter was two or three she would go around the house saying her name, "M-M-M-Maya," just playing with words. I would immediately join in and say, "Yes, that's M-M-M-Mommy and M-M-M-Milk." Because of my informal interventions, she knew phonics essentially before she went to school. I've

since discovered it wasn't necessarily the best model for school success, since she could read and write before entering a very traditional first grade. There are problems in creating a child who is not
content with being bored. She made her statement against basal
reading programs the other day by cutting up the teacher's reading strips.

I recently visited a child-care center where I saw children
pounding nails into a tree stump and having a great time. The
father came in to pick up his daughter and the child said, "Come
see what I'm doing!"

The father joined her at the tree stump and said, "Oh, that's
wonderful."

The father added, "Do you remember what we said those rings
in the tree were for?"

"Yes. To tell how old the tree is."

"Let's count the rings and see how old this tree is."

The point here is that if that child were later put in a tree-
trunk-rich environment, it would appear that she had discovered
what the rings meant on her own when, in essence, the parent had
taught her that.

We need to make sure that when it is important to teach, we
understand it. We need to understand that children may come
with different needs and that we can't allow one methodology to
determine what it is that we are teaching. We have to have a variety
of methodologies. We have to be able to assess broadly. We have to
be able to pull out a direct method or discover a method that
works for the children sitting in front of us.

8. Honor and respect the children's home culture.

This does not mean an all African-American curriculum, necessarily, for African-American children. Most African-American
parents want their children to learn about African Americans, but
they want them to learn about the rest of the world as well. One of
the problems is that there tends to be a denigration of the African-
American culture in many schools and we have to make sure that
doesn't happen.

One of the classes I visited in Baltimore was taught by a wonderful teacher, Stephanie Terry. Stephanie taught first grade and considered herself an Afrocentric teacher. What she did when she taught about libraries, which was in the first-grade curriculum, was teach about the first libraries in Africa. When she taught about health, she taught about Imhotep, an African doctor. It wasn't an issue of not teaching the curriculum as stated, but showing the children how their lives were connected.

I had an opportunity to watch the teacher next to Stephanie, who also tried to use African-American aspects in her curriculum (the school was 100 percent poor African-American kids). This teacher did a lot of research, but when she talked to the children, she said things like, "You see, you see the way you're acting. You could never be Gwendolyn Brooks. You're just too, too, just don't have any sense at all. You just need to sit down and be quiet because you have no ability. You all don't even care about all the work I put into this."

I happened to be at an assembly in which the children were watching Bill Clinton's inauguration. The principal asked, "How many of you think you could be president?" In this 100 percent African-American school, all of Stephanie's kids raised their hands. None of the kids from the classroom next door raised theirs. That really struck me so hard. It's not just the curriculum but the attitudes toward the children that affect what children believe about themselves.

In order to get teachers to understand the wealth and strength of the African-American culture, Gloria Ladson-Billings talks of "having teachers think about what would this country look like today if African Americans just came over on a boat yesterday." There are no right or wrong answers, and the teachers have come up with some interesting points. What they would find if they had just immigrated, just come over on the boat, is there wouldn't be the rich musical heritage provided by the blues, jazz, and gospel. Other teachers suggested that the moral conscience of the nation might not have been heightened without the experience of the civil rights movement. Another teacher suggested that the country would be unrecognizable because we may have failed to grow beyond the thirteen original colonies without the labor of the enslaved African Americans.

The point of that exercise is that as we teach African-American children, we keep in mind the benefits, the virtues, the values, and the contributions of a particular people to this country. We need to keep in mind that these are children from a rich heritage that has brought much to the country.

9. Connect education to a community greater than ourselves.

When many of us were young, we were taught that we weren't just going to school to succeed for ourselves, we were taught that we had to succeed for the group, for the race, for all those people who had come before us. And we owed it to the people who had died, who had worked so hard.

Now our kids are taught that they need an education so they can get a job. So they can personally advance.

Think about the difference between those two perspectives. If you are seeking to excel in order to get a job for yourself and you don't succeed, whom do you disappoint? Just yourself. But if you think about excelling for a community, for your own community, for the country, for people who look like you, if you don't succeed, whom do you fail? You fail a multitude.

There is a much greater significance to believing that your efforts are connected to something larger than yourself than in just believing that I am doing this so that I can get a job and make some money.

One of the things that researchers Shirley Bryce Heathan and Milbrey McLaughlin discovered is that one of the key factors in determining whether children become successsful is the level of connection they feel to some group outside of themselves, some group that is also stirring them onward to be successful. Their research is described in the book *Urban Sanctuaries*.

A challenge

One of the charges that I have as the Benjamin E. Mays Chair holder at Georgia State University is to develop a Center for Urban Educational Excellence. This center, as I see it, will have five components. It will focus (1) on instruction, (2) on parent and community involvement, (3) on school renewal and site-based management, (4) on educational leadership and staff development, and (5) on policy and evaluation. In each of these areas, I would like to see a visiting scholar who would head the effort of research and application. At this point the center consists of only me.

Benjamin Mays, in a commencement address delivered at the University of Liberia in 1960, said, "Education is designed to train the mind to think clearly, logically, and constructively; to train the heart to feel understandingly and sympathetically with the aspirations, the suffering, and the injustices of mankind; to strengthen the will to act in the interest of the common good."

That is what all of us who toil in the vineyards of education must do. Even as Mays himself did it, we must do it without the resources we need. We have our challenge. As Benjamin E. Mays said of his work at Morehouse, "Never have so few done so much with so little."

We all have our marching papers. It's time to march.

Epilogue

As the 1997 Van Andel Educators Institute concluded, we were eager to evaluate the impact and significance of our efforts. Had the institute been a positive, rewarding experience for the participants, all of whom were school superintendents and principals? Did our emphasis on foundational issues have a significant impact? What insights did we gain from the presentations and discussions to guide the future activities and programs at the Van Andel Education Institute?

The responses from participants were very positive and enthusiastic, and included comments such as these:

> This institute was a stimulating, inspiring, thought-provoking experience. It was an opportunity to reflect and be challenged. The selection of speakers was remarkable. Through their unique perspectives, each helped me to understand the challenges facing schools. The theologian, geneticist, sociologist, minority teacher, and engineer focused on the problems and challenges, giving their interpretations of extremely complex social issues. It was a wonderful week— a royal treat.

> The institute was an extraordinary personal and professional experience. Presentations were enlightening and stimulating. Ideas and perspectives were extremely well presented, offering insights into intellectual as well as social problems and issues. The program prompted me to think outside the limits of my job and culture, and to think more deeply about national issues. The institute rates at the top of the personal and professional learning experiences I have been involved with during the past 25 years. A five-star experience.

Though it was rewarding to read such comments, we needed to determine what we had learned during the week about defining the issues in K-12 education and how the Van Andel Education Institute might make a significant contribution. Our review focused on three general categories: cultural issues, leadership, and foundational issues.

Cultural issues

The most difficult issues addressed during the institute were those that relate to character, morals, race, and religion—issues that not only affect society at large but have become serious issues for schools as well. This is not surprising, given the deep cultural divisions in contemporary society.

It was encouraging to find that we were able to discuss these issues in a spirit of civility and mutual respect. It was generally understood that all organizations function more effectively if there is agreement on a broad range of core values and an understanding of how to deal with differences while retaining a sense of unity.

The schedule and format of the week-long institute were not conducive for in-depth discussions on these issues, but there were suggestions that VAEI might well play a role in developing a strategy for definitively addressing them. Though this is an area that one approaches with caution, it is one that offers significant possibilities for future VAEI activities.

Leadership

Superintendents and principals play key leadership roles in our schools. They set the tone and spirit of our schools. They are responsible to ensure that the mission of a school is thoughtfully developed, clearly articulated, and broadly accepted. They must also hire, guide, and encourage the teachers who play such a definitive role in implementing each school's vision.

Focusing on these leaders (and those with the potential to become leaders) rather than on specific educational issues can do much to enhance K-12 education. Placing the focus on leaders and effective organizations is an area in which the Van Andel Education Institute has a continuing interest.

Foundational issues

The Educators Institute was designed to explore foundational issues, not the day-to-day issues facing educators today. As the institute began, we occasionally heard comments such as, "When are we going to address the real issues we face?" By the end of the week we heard, more than once, observations such as, "It was great to set aside our immediate concerns and focus on larger issues." It was evident that our emphasis on foundational issues had struck a resonant chord with participants.

These observations suggest that there is a place in contemporary society, despite its emphasis on the quick fix and short-term goals, for scholarly reflection on the basic issues that impact K-12 education. We believe even more strongly now that providing opportunities for educators to lay aside their immediate responsibilities and spend time in an environment that is conducive to serious reading, discussion, and reflection on the foundational issues of education can make a significant contribution to K-12 education. Because of the positive responses to the 1997 institute, the Van Andel Education Institute is conducting a similar institute during the summer of 1998 as part of the institute's continuing commitment toward K-12 education.

A new venture for VAEI

For some time, VAEI has been looking for a way to make a direct impact on K-12 education. To achieve this goal, the institute has begun work on a program to achieve computer literacy for all teachers and students in one elementary school in Grand Rapids, Michigan, and use this technology to improve learning throughout the curriculum.

This program will be initiated in the summer of 1998. VAEI will lease space in the school, provide computer hardware and software, employ two faculty members, and oversee the computer curriculum. In effect, this will be a school within a school, with the VAEI staff working closely with the teachers and administration in the school.

With gratitude

We look forward to further development and refinement of the role that VAEI can play in K-12 education. We are grateful to all who have helped us in the initial stages of this work and welcome their continued suggestions and counsel.

Gordon J. Van Wylen
Trustee
Van Andel Education Institute

Suggested Reading

Delpit, Lisa D. *Other People's Children*. New York: The Free Press, 1995.

De Pree, Max. *Leadership Is an Art*. New York: Dell, 1989.

——. *Leadership Jazz*. New York: Doubleday, 1992.

——. *Leadership Without Power*. San Francisco: Jossey-Bass, 1997.

Gardner, Howard E. *Creating Minds*. New York: Basic Books, 1993.

——. *Extraordinary Minds*. Basic Books, 1997.

——. *Leading Minds*. New York: Basic Books, 1995.

——. *Multiple Intelligences*. New York: Basic Books, 1993.

——. *The Unschooled Mind*. New York: Basic Books, 1991.

Haynes, Charles. *Finding Common Ground: A First Amendment Guide to Religion in Public Schools*. Nashville: Freedom Forum First Amendment Center at Vanderbilt University, 1994.

Hunter, James Davison. *Culture Wars*. New York: Basic Books, 1991.

Kohl, Herbert, and Colin Greer. *A Call to Character*. New York: Harper Collins, 1995.

Ladson-Billings, Gloria. *Dreamkeepers*. San Francisco: Jossey-Bass, 1994.

McLaughlin, Milbrey. *Urban Sanctuaries*. San Francisco: Jossey-Bass, 1994.

Meilaender, Gilbert. *The Theory and Practice of Virtue*. Notre Dame, Ind.: University of Notre Dame Press, 1984.

Midgley, Mary. *Can't We Make Moral Judgments?* New York: St. Martin's Press, 1991.

Mouw, Richard. *Uncommon Decency*. Downers Grove, Ill.: InterVarsity Press, 1992.

Murnane, Richard, and Frank Levy. *Teaching the New Basic Skills*. New York: The Free Press, 1996.

Plantinga, Jr., Cornelius. *Not the Way It's Supposed to Be: A Breviary of Sin*. Grand Rapids: W. B. Eerdmans, 1995.

Roberts, Robert C. *Spirituality and Human Emotion*. Grand Rapids: W. B. Eerdmans, 1982.

Simon, Caroline. *The Disciplined Heart*. Grand Rapids: W. B. Eerdmans, 1997.

1997
Van Andel Educators Institute

Lecturers

Lisa D. Delpit   Georgia State University
Benjamin E. Mays Chair   Atlanta, Georgia
  of Urban Educational Excellence
Department of Educational Policy Studies

Max De Pree   Herman Miller, Inc.
Chairman Emeritus   Holland, Michigan

Howard E. Gardner   Harvard University
Professor of Education   Cambridge, Massachusetts
Graduate School of Education

James Davison Hunter   University of Virginia
William R. Kenan Jr. Professor   Charlottsville, Virginia
  of Sociology and Religious Studies
Director of The Post-Modernity Project

Ronald M. Latanision   Massachusetts Institute of Technology
Professor of Materials Science   Cambridge, Massachusetts
  and Engineering
Chairman, Council on Primary
  and Secondary Education

Daniel Nathans   Johns Hopkins University
University Professor   Baltimore, Maryland
  of Molecular Biology and Genetics
School of Medicine

Cornelius Plantinga, Jr.   Calvin College
Dean of the Chapel   Grand Rapids, Michigan

Moderators

P. Douglas Kindschi
Dean of Science and Mathematics

Grand Valley State University
Allendale, Michigan

Nancy Miller
Dean for Social Studies

Hope College
Holland, Michigan

Cecil Miskel
Dean, School of Education

University of Michigan
Ann Arbor, Michigan

Participants

Kristin Anderson
Superintendent

Fertile-Beltrami Public Schools
Fertile, Minnesota

Claudia Bach
Superintendent

Milton-Freewater Unified School District #7
Milton-Freewater, Oregon

Kirk Baese
Principal

Ovid-Elsie Area Schools
Elsie, Michigan

Linda M. Beving
Principal

Central High East Campus
Tuscaloosa, Alabama

Marcia Bishop
Superintendent

Holland Public Schools
Holland, Michigan

Robert Buckley
Principal

Flood Brook School
Manchester, Vermont

Kevin Burns
Principal

Eisenhower High School
Blue Island, Illinois

Eugene Cain
Principal

Mid-Michigan Public School Academy
Lansing, Michigan

Regina Campbell
Superintendent

Maine School Administrative District #74
North Anson, Maine

Bruce Chadwick
Superintendent

Saranac Community Schools
Saranac, Michigan

Kathy Chambery
Principal

Burris Laboratory School
Muncie, Indiana

Gary Gelo
Superintendent

Archdiocese of Shreveport
Shreveport, Louisiana

Carmen Hanna
Principal

Van Raalte School
Holland, Michigan

John Herzog
Superintendent

Lutheran High School Association
East Pointe, Michigan

Rochelle Holly
Assistant Superintendent

Archdiocese of Detroit
Detroit, Michigan

Michael Huerth
Principal

Henry High School
Minneapolis, Minnesota

Catherine Keener
Principal

Maude Marshall Elementary School
Oxford, Ohio

Larry Leverett
Superintendent

Plainfield Public Schools
Plainfield, New Jersey

Larry Litman
Headmaster

Mustard Seed School
Hoboken, New Jersey

Patricia A. Lowery
Superintendent

West Branch Area School District
Morrisdale, Pennsylvania

Joseph Mattos
Principal

Joseph H. Bean School
Augusta, Maine

Charles Moore Principal	Hillcrest Elementary School Grand Rapids, Michigan
Joseph Payton Principal	Kalamazoo Central High School Kalamazoo, Michigan
Elizabeth Rudenga Department of Education	Trinity Christian College Palos Heights, Illinois
Douglas Sasse Superintendent	Gratiot-Isabella Regional Education District Ithaca, Michigan
John Simpson Superintendent	Ann Arbor Public Schools Ann Arbor, Michigan
Joe M. Tolley Principal	Silverado High School Victorville, California
Daniel Vander Ark Executive Director	Christian Schools International Grand Rapids, Michigan
Jack C. Van Newkirk Superintendent	York City School District York, Pennsylvania
Renee R. Williams Superintendent	Benton Harbor Schools Benton Harbor, Michigan